SEE THE  GOOD

SEE
THE
GOOD

FINDING GRACE, GRATITUDE, AND OPTIMISM IN EVERY DAY

ZACH WINDAHL

a division of Baker Publishing Group
Minneapolis, Minnesota

Published by Bethany House Publishers
11400 Hampshire Avenue South
Minneapolis, Minnesota 55438
www.bethanyhouse.com

Bethany House Publishers is a division of
Baker Publishing Group, Grand Rapids, Michigan

Printed in the United States of America

Library of Congress Cataloging-in-Publication Data
Names: Windahl, Zach, author.
Title: See the good : finding grace, gratitude, and optimism in every day /
    Zach Windahl.
Description: Minneapolis, Minnesota : Bethany House Publishers, a division
    of Baker Publishing Group, [2022]
Identifiers: LCCN 2022024697 | ISBN 9780764241000 (paper) | ISBN
    9780764241420 (casebound) | ISBN 9781493439423 (ebook)
Subjects: LCSH: Christian life. | Joy—Religious aspects—Christianity.
Classification: LCC BV4501.3 .W5569 2022 | DDC 248.4—dc23/
    eng/20220708
LC record available at https://lccn.loc.gov/2022024697

Cover design by Dan Pitts

Interior illustrations by Zach Windahl

Baker Publishing Group publications use paper produced from sustainable
forestry practices and post-consumer waste whenever possible.

22 23 24 25 26 27 28   7 6 5 4 3 2 1

TO GISELA.

Thank you for making every moment
worth remembering.
I will never stop saying "I love you."

Contents

Foreword

IF YOU'RE ANYTHING LIKE ME, it doesn't take much these days to hear about how badly things are going. Turn on the TV, open your phone, or strike up a conversation with the person in line next to you at the grocery store, and chances are you will hear about the poor state of the world. In fact, it seems to me, most people are more acutely aware of the world's worsening state than ever before. From pandemics to politics, there is a feeling that things are going from bad to worse. And for so many reasons, things are pretty tough for a lot of people right now. Divisions socially and politically are causing major stress and problems; people have lost loved ones and suffered in so many ways over the past few years . . . It would be very reasonable to understand why people feel the way they do.

I have been close to and witnessed some of the most terrible experiences in recent history. I have seen natural disasters, wars, famine, and other horrific events firsthand that make our reality seem extremely pessimistic. Yet I am consistently surprised to see people in the darkest of situations rise up to bring light to those around them. I have seen it time and again all around the world. When I assume things should only be heavy and hard, there are people who are able to see things from a different perspective and, in the face of overwhelming adversity, focus on the good to be found in life. Have you met any of these people? The ones who seem to always have a glint of joy in their eyes, with laughter never too far away? These are the people others look to in the hardest of times, and the resilience that hallmarks their lives seems to come from somewhere other than their circumstances.

My experience and friendship with Zach Windahl has shown me that he is one of those people. The kind of person who doesn't gloss over or avoid difficult situations, but who embraces the difficult, knowing full well the hope found in those valley moments of our lives. In the following pages, Zach helps us understand how and why we should acknowledge the hard parts of life but choose to also see the good, and live a positive life in response. The longer I live, and the more people I meet, I am learning what it means to see life as a gift to be grateful for. Zach and those like him who have discovered the reasons for focusing on the good are willing to also respond to the good in life with gratitude, and step forward with grit and determination to make our world a better place. For when you are able to see the good and find life as a gift, it truly makes you want to give something back in return.

As you read this book, be inspired and encouraged to see your life and the lives of others around you from a new perspective. In doing so, I hope you will learn to give back to life as you find ways to receive what it is already trying to give you.

—Bob Goff
New York Times bestselling author

PART ONE

CHANGING THE WAY WE SEE

CHAPTER 1

Shifting Our Perspective

"MOM IS SICK."

At four years old, I didn't grasp the depth those three words held.

She probably has a stomachache, I thought. *If she drinks some ginger ale, she'll be better soon.*

Little did I know that my mother had been diagnosed with stage 4 ovarian cancer. The doctor sent her home with a 5 percent chance to live.

The thing about such a fresh diagnosis is that you would never have known what was going on internally, because on the outside she looked fine. At least for a while. But after a few months, the weight began to slide off and she became skin and bones.

I couldn't recognize my own mother anymore.

One evening as she was in her room at the hospital, she was visited by our family friend, Papa Don, who came equipped with a Bible and a word to share. Even though my mom had grown up in the church, she was taught from tradition instead of being invited into a relationship with Jesus. Relationship with Christ is essential. And so that night, on her hospital bed, everything changed.

My mom was healed spiritually and was filled with a hope that couldn't be shaken. She knew where she was headed, no matter the outcome of the cancer. And as her treatment progressed, so did her physical healing. A few months later she was cancer-free.

But her war with cancer didn't stop there. And neither did healing and hope.

Over the next ten years she battled on—through a tumor around her sciatic nerve, colon cancer that required three-quarters of her colon to be removed, and to top it off, breast cancer with a double mastectomy and reconstructive surgery. From the ages of four to fifteen, I saw my mom cycle in and out of the hospital, never knowing if she was going to make it.

I guess you could say my childhood was unique. Different.

The best thing that could have happened to us, actually.

Because do you want to know what really shaped me down to my bones? The fact that I never saw my mom upset with God or depressed or adopting a "poor me" mentality. No, the entire time, she found a way to see the good and reminded me how much worse life could be. I mean, she could have been dead. But she wasn't.

She was alive.

I was alive.

You, reading this, are alive.

Some people weren't blessed with that opportunity.

But maybe an optimistic outlook on life isn't natural for you, like it was for my mom. Maybe you're angry with God. Or maybe you feel like you just can't catch a break. I know how that goes. I also know there are mindset shifts and habits we can incorporate to help each of us lead a more grace-filled, hope-filled life; I believe this book will help point you in the right direction.

Just think what would happen if we opened our eyes to all that God is doing in our midst—the good in our personal lives and in the greater world.

What if we started sharing those stories with others?

What if we began to help people see God in ways they never knew of before?

It's going to change your life and the lives of others. I promise.

Better or Worse?

Since the age of four, I have been given a forced education in how joy works and was introduced to the importance of gratitude toward life because it was almost taken away before my eyes.

I am a routine guy. Super type-A, and a 3 wing 2 on the Enneagram. Yeah, you know the type. Everything planned out. Every morning is the same:

I wake up to my alarm at 7 a.m.

Shower.

Clean my glasses and grab my Bible.

Take my dog, Nyla, outside to do her business.

We eat breakfast together, which is really just me chugging a protein shake because it takes her seventeen seconds to devour her food.

And then I sit on our couch to read my Bible and share a thought or two on social media.

Same thing. Every day.

One day, I decided to post two polls on my Instagram Story. I was a little curious that day after seeing so many anxiety-driven posts online.

Poll one:
Do you think the state of the world is getting better or worse?

Poll two:
As Christians, do you think it's getting easier or harder to be a Christian?

Honestly, I don't really know what I was expecting the answers to be. But after twenty-four hours, I was shocked by the responses.

84 percent of people said the world was getting worse.
81 percent said it was getting harder to be a Christian.

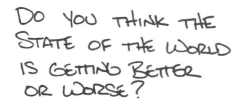

I was astonished at people's perspectives.

I sat there and just didn't understand. I wondered how so many Christians could have such a negative outlook on the future. Do I not have the same outlook on life that most people do? I thought about this for a while and was flooded with emotions.

I was so confused, a bit sad and curious—and pretty angry. Angry because I couldn't understand the surprisingly negative results of the polls and because I had so many follow-up questions that wouldn't fit in the character limit of the Questions box on Instagram.

I couldn't just sit there and wonder, though. I needed to know how this happened. I needed to do something about it. *We* need to do something about this.

So I began my discovery process as normal, with a simple question: *Why?*

Here are some of the reasons people voted the way they did:

"We are in the last days!"
"We are experiencing censorship and pastors being arrested."
"Christians are being hated and everyone hates God."
"Churches could lose tax exemption status in the next two years."
"Pop culture makes the world more accepting of sin."
"Christians are getting all the wrong labels, and lies are being told."
"World views are moving more away from the Bible."
"Because nobody loves anymore, it's all about judgment and hate."
"The gospel isn't being preached."
"Society is full of lawlessness and temptation."
"Christian ethics are more hated than ever."
"I don't think it's getting better or worse. It's just different."

Those responses are all real concerns and problems people all over are dealing with. I'm happy everyone shared their thoughts with me; they allowed me a glimpse of why people answered the poll the way they did. And I am in no way trying to downplay the bad circumstances people are seeing and experiencing everywhere.

But I still didn't really get it. How did we get here?

We Are So Bored

If you want a great burger in Minneapolis, go to a spot called Nolo's. They have this duck burger that will knock your socks off.

The other day when I was there, my friend Ethan ordered a plate of sauteed shishito peppers for my friends Tiago, Luke, and me. He said that one in twenty peppers will be so hot you lose your breath.

Don't threaten me with a good time.

As we worked our way through the tray of peppers, flinching with every bite, I brought up the results of my Instagram poll and how it was messing with my head. How I couldn't comprehend why so many people thought the world was getting worse.

I shared stats such as how, in the last twenty-five years alone,

- world hunger has declined 40 percent;
- the child mortality rate has been cut in half;
- extreme poverty has fallen by three-quarters; and
- 88 percent of children have been vaccinated against at least one disease.[1]

Looking at this from a macro perspective, the world is trending positively. Wouldn't you agree?

So I asked the guys what they thought. Luke said, "I think it's because we are so bored and we need things to complain about." I thought about his response for a second and, well, I completely agree.

We are just so bored.

And we lack perspective.

Dentistry and a Printing Press

I was selling shirts at a Christian music festival the day after I got my wisdom teeth removed. It was hot, hot, and I was hungry, hungry, but the only thing I could consume while my mouth was healing were meal-replacement shakes. And considering that I was at a Christian music festival on a hot summer day, instead of at my home with a refrigerator, my shakes were warm. And strawberry flavored. I'm not sure if the strawberry made it worse or not, but those things were definitely curdled by the end of the day, and I had to choke them down.

As nasty as that may have been though, how nice is it that when you need to have your wisdom teeth removed, you can drive down the street to the dentist, get drugged up, have the dentist take them out, and a few days later the swelling is down and you're all healed. Praise God for that!

What do you think happened two hundred years ago if you had wisdom teeth issues? Like, you need to realize that Novocaine was invented in 1905. What do you think they did to numb the pain before local anesthetics were developed? Anything? Rub a random leaf that they foraged on it?

To take it a step further, how do you think dental surgeries took place during Old Testament times? Yikes.

Think of it: It's the middle of summer in 2500 BC. The world powers at the time are Egypt and Babylon in Mesopotamia, controlling what is known as the Fertile Crescent.

To understand the region a little better, make a peace sign with your left hand.

Your forearm is the Red Sea.

Your middle finger is the Gulf of Suez.

Your pointer finger is the Gulf of Aqaba. To the left of your hand is Egypt.

Between your fingers is the Sinai Peninsula.

And to the right of your hand is Saudi Arabia.

Above that is Mesopotamia and where the Promised Land would end up being—modern-day Jordan, Israel, etc.

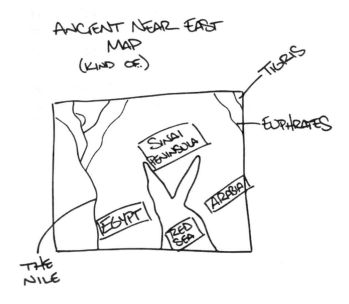

Three massive rivers ran through the land: the Nile through Egypt, and the Tigris and Euphrates through Mesopotamia.

This land was special. And the rivers are what made it extravagant.

Nearly every spring, all three rivers would overflow and flood the land, resulting in a plentiful harvest for all of the people groups. They believed that the more they sacrificed to their gods, the greater the flood and the more abundant the harvest would be. We'll talk more about this later, but I wanted you to have a brief understanding for now.

So, back to the vision.

It's the summer of 2500 BC. You are preparing a meal for your family by grinding wheat with a mortar and pestle that were passed down by your parents and are looking a little rough around the edges. What you don't realize as you're grinding is that a small chunk of rock broke off the pestle into the dough mixture. Blind to the tragedy that is about to ensue, you knead the dough into cakes for dinner and begin cooking them over the fire. The smell of goodness flows through the air, calling your family to gather for a bite of what you've been slaving away at. But moments like these with the entire family together make all of the work completely worth it.

You sit back.

Your spouse smiles. Your daughter laughs as your son cracks another joke.

This is peace. This is harmony.

You grab your plate, take a bite, and immediately regret using that old pestle and mortar, as the small chip of rock just broke your lower molar.

OUCH.

Now what?

The good news is that archaeologists have uncovered mummies from the same time period that have holes in their teeth and jaws from dental surgeries.

The bad news is that there was no anesthetic or laughing gas.

Dental surgery wasn't preventative for them as it is for us today. They only brought out the drills when there was a real problem. Think of how excruciating the pain and discomfort would have been with no numbing cream. At the same time, think of how terrible the pain would be if you broke a tooth and didn't do anything about it. It was a lose-lose situation.

When it comes to dentistry, things are definitely better now. I don't do well with blood, and shivers just crawled up my spine as I typed this, thinking about getting my wisdom teeth ripped out.

I know they're called wisdom teeth, but that doesn't sound very wise to me.

And don't even get me started with circumcision.

There's a type of literature in the Bible called Wisdom literature. It's all about helping you live life. Not necessarily rules, but tips on how to live well.

Like, "For lack of guidance a nation falls, but victory is won through many advisers,"[2] and "Commit your actions to the LORD, and your plans will succeed."[3] Stuff like that.

I'm a big fan.

I'm so grateful that we have this ancient wisdom available at our fingertips, whether in a printed Bible or on your phone. (You're definitely holier if you have the real thing, but that's neither here nor there.)

Did you know that it was only five hundred years ago that the first Bible was printed in English? You couldn't just go and buy a Bible at a store. In the past, you would have had to write it out. My hand cramps just thinking about it.

Not only that, but back in the day, you definitely couldn't live out your faith in public as we are able to do in many parts of the world today. It wasn't because a few people didn't like Christians so they were being persecuted. No, *Rome* hated Christians. Like, the *entire world power* Rome. From what a lot of early church scholars believe, the Romans didn't really understand Christianity, especially as it moved away from Judaism and became more Hellenized. Christians were a threat. They were saying that a new kingdom had arrived and was taking over.

Other mystery cults were spreading at the time as well, such as the cult of Bacchus and the cult of Mithras. These cult followers would worship in secret and have meals together, encouraging one another in their faith, just as the Christians did. Not only that, but they would eat the flesh of their god in the form of bread and drink the blood in the form of wine, as we do in our Eucharist. So when the

Roman government was looking at these various groups of people, they couldn't tell the difference, and Christians were persecuted the same as the rest.

Rome had an emperor for a few years named Nero, who was the worst. He would feed Christians to lions for entertainment. He would also dip them in oil, impale them, and light them on fire to be used as lanterns at his dinner parties.

And we're complaining about our churches losing their tax-exempt status. Come on. That's a slap in the face to our Christian lineage.

We have it so good.

There are so many things to be grateful for.

I love how, when I asked the question "Why?" about the poll results, one person responded, "I don't think it's getting better or worse. It's just different."

I agree with that.

Maybe I needed to adjust my question, because the answer isn't binary. It's complex. We need to muddy the waters a little bit.

Is it getting better? Yes, it is trending positive.

Is it getting worse? Also, yes. Many things are terrible right now.

So I guess it's kind of like asking, "How was 2020?" or "How was your childhood?"

There were a lot of things that were good and bad, depending on how you look at it.

It's true that many bad things are going on, like racial injustice, the threat of nuclear weapons, our mental health crisis, our earth crisis, and division in the church. But there are also countless things to be grateful for, such as modern dentistry and the availability of Bibles, for starters.

We get to decide what story we're telling. God is literally allowing us to participate in the ongoing creation of the world.

These are the days the church was created for. What an extraordinary thing to be alive and have this experience. What else could we want?

Almost losing my mom during my most developmental years taught me a lot of life lessons, but they can be summed up into two main things:

God is good.

And all of life is a gift.

CHAPTER 2

You Decide the Story

YOU AND I DON'T NEED to go on a missions trip to help people.

And we don't need to work for a church.

Neither makes us more holy.

My wife grew up going to the Dominican Republic every year with her family and friends. Every. Single. Year. They went so often that they became friends with the employees of the resort and would bring an extra suitcase full of clothes and toys for those families on every trip. Hearing stories of how those minor acts impacted the employees' lives in such tremendous ways really pumped me up. And the fact that the Dominican Republic is one of the most beautiful places ever made it even more attractive.

So G and I decided we were going to create new traditions with our group of friends from all over the country. One week each year we would all fly to a distant location and have an absolute blast together.

The first year we chose the Dominican Republic, because it was comfortable and we would be able to host our friends, showing them what we had fallen in love with.

When you visit tourist destinations, there are always excursions you can participate in around the area. G's dad kept telling me about the "boogies" and how they were by far the best addition to your trip. To tell you the truth, I had no idea what boogies were, but everyone else's excitement got me fired up, so I was sold.

The only hang-up was that the boogies were popular, and we didn't think we could get a reservation.

My friend Brentom thought otherwise. This dude's faith is like nothing I've ever witnessed. Sometimes I think he's an angel. I'm still not positive if my theory is right or wrong. So Brentom—covered in favor—floated over to the counter, and two minutes later he walked back with a reservation in hand, like it was nothing.

Praise God.

That afternoon it was going down.

At three we met in the lobby, awaiting our shuttle. The front-desk worker had told us to dress for the mess, so we really looked like a ragtag group—bandanas over our faces, hats down over our eyebrows, all black clothing.

I wasn't sure if we were robbing a bank or going to play in the mud.

Our shuttle arrived and we were loaded in like cattle, preparing for only God knows what. The person next to me, wearing a Gucci bag and sandals, definitely had been tricked into this.

"ARE YOU READY FOR SOME BOOGIEEEEESSSSSS?!?!" called the shuttle driver over the loudspeaker.

And we all started chanting—barking, basically. I don't know, man, my inner primate came out or something. For whatever reason, my friend Nate gets me so fired up, I was about to hang out of the windows.

We were ready.

The shuttle drove us through different villages to get to our location. Along the way we saw poverty like I had never witnessed before. Small cement houses with no doors or windows. Malnourished dogs walking alongside the road. Garbage everywhere.

But the people . . . they didn't look much different from us. I'm not sure what I expected of people living in such poverty, but I didn't expect to see smiles and dancing or joy and laughter. Yes, they may not have had a lot of material items, but they were rich in character.

We pulled into our destination, which was a small open-walled building surrounded by "boogies," aka dune buggies, aka four-wheelers with cages.

It was game time.

We were paired off to different boogies. I teamed up with Nate.

As we were pulling out of the parking lot, a group who just finished their excursion was pulling in. And let me tell you, these guys were *filthy*. Absolutely covered in mud from head to toe.

I thought I was prepared, but now I knew: I was definitely not prepared.

We slowly started making our way through the streets. Kids chased after us trying to sell us flowers and drawings for a dollar each. I love art, so of course I bought one and emptied my pockets as a tip.

The tour guide started moving faster, so I folded the drawing and tucked it away before I could see what it was. But I knew it was going to be good.

Nate was driving at this point. All of a sudden, we took a sharp right turn into a mud pit, and the dirty water parted around our boogie like a Red Sea moment before crashing down. My glasses were immediately brown, and my shirt was so soaked I couldn't clean the lenses off. But I needed to see, so into my mouth they went.

For the next forty-five minutes, Nate and I switched off driving—plowing through mud puddles, spinning around, and having the time of our lives. My hair was so blown back I felt like we were in a rocket.

When things calmed down, our guide began directing us back to the drop-off spot, and we were finished for the day. What stuck with me most was the joy radiating from the kids we drove past.

It can be so easy to look at people with less than us and think about all the ways we have it better than they do. But I know a lot of people with a whole lot of stuff who are pretty miserable.

When we got back to the resort, I unfolded the drawing I had purchased from that kid. In the middle of the torn notebook paper was a yellow heart with flower petals coming out from all around it. I couldn't stop staring at it with a smile from ear to ear.

In the middle of the mess, covered in dirt, surrounded by what many people would call poverty, I was the one being impacted by God. When I thought I was doing something to help this boy, he was really helping me. That boy offered me a drawing and a big smile. He reminded me that love can be spread in any circumstance, clean or dirty. He helped me to see the good.

You Decide the Story

Almost every situation has two sides to it.

We can think in one way and be pessimistic.

Or we can think in another way and be optimistic.

Neither is necessarily superior.

But how we view God, our role on earth, and what the future holds impacts our perspective on life and how we will see things. God allows us to choose.

I personally hold a very positive outlook on the future. I tend to be quite optimistic, and I believe that every day it is our role to love others to the best of our ability.

What's fascinating to me is that many Christians today have a negative outlook on the future because of what someone told them about the book of Revelation or what the news told them or because they just feel everything is hopeless at this point.

I'm here to tell you that it doesn't have to be that way.

It's okay to go against the grain.

It's okay to disagree with people.

You get to decide the story you're telling.

We will explore in a minute how there has been such tremendous growth in the areas of science, technology, and communication over the last few decades alone, but there is this strange mindset among so many Christians that they don't associate with the "world." This is largely because of the saying in Christian circles that "Christians are in the world, but not of the world." We focus so much on the spiritual but lack ownership of the material reality we participate in every day. We identify with another place, so we feel it's no longer our responsibility to look after the one where we are currently living.

God is present in the material world just as much as he is present in the spiritual world. Our role remains the same. To bring heaven to earth, now.

OUR ROLES REMAIN
THE SAME :

TO BRING HEAVEN
TO EARTH

God made us on purpose.

He made trees on purpose.

He made coffee beans on purpose.

He made relationships and family and beauty on purpose.

We are here, alive, surrounded by goodness, and it's all on purpose.

Do you know how improbable it is that you and I are alive? The odds are 1 in 400 trillion.[1] But we care more about reality TV because we are so bored with our own lives.

In the Christian and Jewish tradition, prophets used to be called "seers" because they helped people see things differently. They helped people see things from God's perspective and not from their own.

As Christianity has progressed, especially in America, the view of prophecy has become fairly distorted. We think it's only used to predict the future, and when we read the Old Testament prophets, they're difficult to understand, so we lump them together and claim everything they said was just pointing to Jesus anyway.

This is true and legitimizes the need for the Old Testament in the first place. But prophecy in itself functions differently. Prophets weren't concerned with the sub-level meaning of their prophetic words. They were focusing on their current situation, reading the times, and understanding their present reality.

The prophet's role is to reject the given narrative about what creation is moving toward and reimagine it in light of the community they are working with. Then and there. Here and now.

The doom-and-gloom mentality many Christians hold today does not accurately reflect the reality of what it means to be a Christian in the twenty-first century. This entire mindset needs to be challenged.

We need to wake up.

God is alive and active.

How heartbreaking to miss out on everything he is doing around us just because we are so caught up in fear and worry. What a terrible witness to non-believers.

We get to decide the story we are telling people.

And it needs to be rewritten.

Negativity Bias

One of the greatest habits we can adopt is the ancient tradition of gratitude. As basic as that may sound, incorporating a practice of gratitude into our daily lives is one of the best things for our mental health.

University of California, Davis, psychologist Robert Emmons is an expert in the science of gratitude, and he defines gratitude as "an affirmation of the goodness in one's life and the recognition that the sources of this goodness lie at least partially outside the self."[2] He continues by arguing that gratitude is actually healthy and good for you. He says that we are made by God to be grateful and that when we are, we experience God's blessings, including happiness and contentment.

But gratitude doesn't come easily for a lot of people. We need to work toward it. Research has shown that 50 percent of our emotional disposition is genetic, which means that change is hard for a lot of people.[3] Anxiety, depression, and fear can be crippling. People are struggling with mental health in numbers we've never experienced before, or at least had words for.

More recently, neuroscientists have found that we are all born with something called a "negativity bias"—the tendency to register and dwell on negative experiences more than we do positive experiences of the same intensity. Our brain registers experiences in order to learn from them; the negative ones often help us identify when something is dangerous, and in the future protect ourselves. It's a really incredible thing.

Until it isn't.

Until our brains are always on high alert for dangers, and that influences us to always be thinking negatively.

Positive experiences, on the other hand, are often forgotten before the day ends because of this fight-or-flight mentality. We have experienced a bunch of great things in a day, but the stress of the negative overpowers the positive.

So where does this come from?

It goes back—way, way back—to our ancestors on the plains of Africa, not aware if something is hiding behind the next bush. Always on edge. There's a tree, there's a butterfly, there's a flower, all of these beautiful things, but at any moment a lion could jump out. Negativity bias is simply your body protecting you from danger.

It can be a positive thing, to an extent. If you're walking on a mountainside trail, your fear of falling will keep you present and aware of your surroundings. We just can't allow that voice of fear and negativity to have too loud a voice in instances that aren't truly life-threatening.

Sometimes it is hard to make that mental shift and go against our nature. But it's one of the best things we can train our minds to do—not to ignore the reality of what is happening, but to address it and experience it from a big-picture perspective instead of letting small things ruin our entire day.

We spilled coffee on our pants?

We got cut off in traffic?

Our partner gave us attitude this morning?

Are we really going to allow such things to mess with us all day?

If we expect bad things to happen, they're going to happen. Likewise, if we expect good things to happen, they're going to happen. Most days aren't to the extreme one way or another. Most days are pretty average. But one negative experience can make an average day seem bad instead of just being average.

Yes, there is so much to be upset about in the world.

But there is also so much to be amazed at.

So much wonder and awe all around, if we know where to look for it.

And I believe that's our role as believers: to find God in everything, to find the good all around us and call it out. And to share it with others, just as the prophets of the Old Testament were trying to do.

We are supposed to be spreading heaven on earth.

Rewiring

The worst thing we could do is believe that tomorrow is just going to be the same as today, or worse.

In the book of Exodus, we learn about a man named Moses. At a time when the Israelites were multiplying at an alarming rate, Pharaoh commanded that all male babies be drowned in the Nile River (remember the big river in Egypt we talked about earlier, along the Fertile Crescent?).

But Moses' mother couldn't grasp the idea of her baby being killed, so she placed him in a basket in the Nile as a means of protection.

Pharaoh's daughter found the Hebrew baby and decided to adopt him, raising him in Egyptian royalty.

As Moses grew older, he had more power and authority among the people. Although outwardly he might have looked happy, and other Hebrews might have been jealous of the life Moses had, he was experiencing an internal battle. He was witnessing brutality among his people day in and day out. You see, the Hebrews were slaves to the Egyptians. And it was the Hebrews' role to make bricks.

One after another.

Brick.

Brick.

Brick.

The story goes on to describe the day when Moses became upset and killed an Egyptian guard for beating one of the Hebrews. When Moses realized that somebody had found out, he fled the country out of fear.

Fast-forward nearly forty years later, God used Moses to perform ten miracles in front of the new Pharaoh, in hopes of letting his people go free from slavery.

The first was turning the Nile River water into blood.
The second was an attack of frogs.
The third was lice.

The fourth gnats.
The fifth was the killing of all Egyptian livestock.
Then came boils.
And hail.
Swarming locusts.
Complete darkness for three days.
And finally, the killing of every Egyptian's firstborn son.

The last one pushed Pharaoh over the edge, and he allowed all the Hebrews to go free. But four hundred years of slavery doesn't disappear from a people overnight. It took the Hebrews forty years in the wilderness just to get the Egyptian mindset out of them.

Think about it for a second. It was now:

Brick.

Brick.

No more bricks.

Their worth was no longer found in how many bricks they could produce. Their worth was now found in the simple fact that they were God's chosen people. Imagine how jarring that would have been for them; having to change their deeply rooted mindset in an instant was almost impossible.

And the same is true for us.

We can get so caught up in all that is happening around us and give in to the negativity bias we are constantly battling that a real change of pace can be tough. We need to be deconditioned from our normal way of thinking and renew our minds every morning.

Paul tells the Philippian church,

> Always be full of joy in the Lord. I say it again—rejoice! Let everyone see that you are considerate in all you do. Remember, the Lord is coming soon.
>
> Don't worry about anything; instead, pray about everything. Tell God what you need, and thank him for all he has done. Then you will experience God's peace, which exceeds anything we can understand. His peace will guard your hearts and minds as you live in Christ Jesus.
>
> And now, dear brothers and sisters, one final thing. Fix your thoughts on what is true, and honorable, and right, and pure, and lovely, and admirable. Think about things that are excellent and worthy of praise. Keep putting into practice all you learned and received from me—everything you heard from me and saw me doing. Then the God of peace will be with you.
>
> Philippians 4:4–9 NLT

Do this.

And God will be with you.

Think about these things.

And God will be with you.

As believers, we need to learn how to rewire our minds to be more like Christ. To see things from his perspective and not our own. Your lens profoundly impacts how you interact with life, how you love God, and how you love those around you.

To live as a Christian means to expand heaven on earth today and have faith for a fully renewed world in the future, for everyone.

The Real State of the World

So many Christians today are stuck in the mindset that the world is falling apart. That the "good old days" are long gone and now we are spiraling toward destruction. It doesn't help that we are exposed to nearly five thousand advertisements every day and that most news stations rarely focus on the good taking place because it isn't as sellable.

But are things really getting worse? Let's look at the facts.

It is clear that prior to 2020 and the emergence of COVID-19, data drawn from Our World in Data (OWID) and reported on by various news outlets gave the resounding verdict that the world is, in fact, getting better. Dylan Matthews, writing for *Vox*, presented twenty-three maps from OWID and other sources, displaying the improvement in four major areas:[4]

Economic Progress

1. Extreme poverty, hunger, and child labor all have declined.
2. In developed countries, people have more leisure time.
3. In the U.S., the percentage of income spent on food has dropped.

Health

1. Life expectancy is increasing.
2. Child mortality and death in childbirth have decreased.
3. In the U.S., smoking and teen pregnancy rates are down.

Peace and Security

1. Over the long term, homicide rates in Western Europe have fallen dramatically.
2. In the U.S., homicide rates are also down, and violent crime is dropping.
3. The supply of nuclear weapons has been reduced.

Government, Social Services, and Technology

1. More people now live in a democracy.
2. More people are going to school longer, and literacy is up.
3. Internet access is increasing.
4. Solar energy is getting cheaper.

The list goes on and on. Yet despite these societal improvements, perception by many is that things are actually getting worse.

Max Roser, writing for OWID, discusses this misperception. Regarding global poverty, he writes, "The majority of people—52%—believe that the share of people in extreme poverty is rising. The opposite is true. In fact, the share of people living in extreme poverty across the world has been declining for two centuries, and in the last 20 years this positive development has been faster than ever before."[5]

He also notes that 61 percent of those surveyed believe, contrary to fact, that either child mortality has stayed the same or has increased. He goes on to argue that misperceptions regarding these issues "feeds into a general discontent about how the world is changing," with only 6 percent of those surveyed in the U.S. saying the world is getting better. Moreover, 29 percent of those surveyed believe living conditions will decline in the future.

If you drive around the country of Bhutan, you might come across road signs that say things like, "Life is a journey. Complete it!" and other various encouragements, because in the 1970s they made a decision to change the way they viewed the health of their country.

Instead of measuring progress by the gross domestic product (GDP), which is what most countries do, they decided to focus on measuring the Gross National Happiness by looking at the "spiritual, physical, social and environmental health of its citizens and natural environment."[6] The Bhutan government cares more about the well-being of its citizens than the advancement of political power.

And what is the result?

People are happier.

They are living longer.

Their natural resources are thriving.

All from making one simple change of focus.

When I was a kid, I thought I was the coolest. I had a serious obsession with rap music, and my friend Courtney had an older brother with every rap CD imaginable. Needless to say, every time I went to her house, I was in heaven.

Back in the day, if you had a boom box, you could record a CD onto a cassette tape, but you had to sit and listen to the entire thing while the song was transferring over. That was no problem for me since Courtney's brother had all the music I could ever want.

One small problem: My parents wouldn't let me listen to most of them.

So I got sneaky. I would record it all onto a cassette tape and then write either "Spice Girls" or "Hanson" on the outside so they had no idea. It was genius.

I also thought I was super cool because I was an inline skater. That's just a fancy way of saying that I rollerbladed around the skate park, pretending I could grind down rails and go off jumps—neither of which I was all that good at, but I would put my headphones in and jam out for hours.

While my intake consisted of garbage, the outside looked cute and harmless.

This tends to be the case with a lot of content we consume today, especially on social media and in the news. While every post and every story shows how bad things are in the world, we don't realize how they are impacting our approach to life because to us, we're just staying on top of what's happening globally.

My mom always said to me, "Zach, remember, garbage in, garbage out."

I hated that phrase because of how convicting it was.

But it's true.

What do we fill our minds with that manifests itself in a negative way?

Maybe it's the news, maybe it's a friend who is obsessed with conspiracy theories, maybe it's a certain type of music, or a relationship.

We wonder why we are anxious or have a negative outlook on life, but we never perform an audit of what we are consuming.

Let's get better at that. Let's replace the negativity with content that is going to boost our faith and encourage us to impact the world in a more positive way.

Our perspective is so incredibly powerful. What you look for you will find, whether that's a state of paradise or a bunch of fog. We can't overlook the good things happening in our daily lives, even in the midst of difficulties.

We are all part of something so much bigger than just what is right in front of us. We are part of an ever-changing landscape that is constantly improving in numerous ways. It's all about how we look at it.

I'm not going to spend time looking in the rearview mirror of my life. I know what I'm called to do and I'm going to use everything in my being to spread heaven on earth in the now. I'm not going to ignore the bad news; I'm going to use it as inspiration to find a solution.

You and I are called to bring change,
to bring kingdom,
to show the goodness of God.

Because you and I are not like the rest of the world.

We are new creations.

CHAPTER 3

New Creation

OUR CREATION STORY does not involve violence.

You and I were not created to make the lives of the "gods" easier.

The one, true God created man and said it was "very good."

But during the time of early Hebrew history, people were bombarded with different explanations for why they were alive—what the point was for everything they experienced.

Imagine being a Hebrew, questioning life after being violently conquered by the Babylonians and taken away from their homeland. Back then, they probably would have been taught what is known as the Babylonian creation story, which would have been told in a similar fashion as this:

A long, long time ago there were younger gods and older gods. Apsu and Tiamat were two of the older gods, and they were beginning to clash.

Apsu was the god of freshwater. Tiamat was the goddess of saltwater. The two were constantly mixing together in this uncreated state. A little saltwater here, a little freshwater there. Blending together and creating chaos. (Sound familiar?)

The younger gods were acting out against the older gods and not respecting the social order of the time, so Apsu responds violently to their idiocy, assuming Tiamat would back him up, considering they were the older gods of the time. But Tiamat decided to join in with the younger gods in hopes of full supremacy.

Tiamat spent time building an army of underworld beasts to represent her and the proposed new world order. These dudes were mean-looking and would scare even the toughest person out of their socks.

The older gods didn't know what to do because they couldn't find anybody on their side strong enough to fight against the chaotic army of scoundrels Tiamat organized.

Until one day, when Marduk stepped on the scene.

He was powerful.

He was a leader.

He had everything he needed to take on Tiamat.

There was one stipulation. Marduk only agreed to fight on behalf of the older gods as long as he was made head of the pantheon.

The gods agreed.

It was time to prepare for battle.

With a mace in one hand and thunderbolts in the other, Marduk was ready to attack. He covered his body in fire and held a net to grab Tiamat if she tried any funny business.

Marduk organized all four winds.

North.
South.
East.
West.

Converged into a cyclone that doubled as a chariot to ride into battle, Marduk bypasses the army and goes straight for Tiamat, the chaotic waters who were now in the form of a sea dragon. (What?! Yeah, I know. Weird.)

Marduk throws the cyclone into Tiamat's mouth, opening it up far enough to shoot an arrow down her throat into her heart.

As crazy as it sounds, it worked. Marduk, for sure, played it off like he knew what he was doing, but I guarantee he was a little surprised as well.

He was now the victor.

The savior of the world.

The rightful head of the pantheon.

And it was time to re-create order in the world.

Marduk cut open the body of Tiamat from head to toe, split it right in two, and used half of her corpse to create the cosmos. From there, Marduk arranged the stars, the moon, and the constellations.

He wasn't through. He and all of the gods were sick of working, so he went after Kingsu, Tiamat's partner, and drained his blood to create man to work on their behalf.

The first city was then built: Babylon.

And the Hebrew who had asked the question about life would have been told, "And that's where we are today—Babylon, the greatest city in the world, and our god, Marduk, is the most powerful there is."

It's a wild story. And for ancient people, it had a major influence on their outlook on life. Can you even imagine if we believed human beings came out of bloodshed and divine violence? How would that impact the way we value and treat human life? Astonishing.

The origin story I just shared is called the Enuma Elish, and it was spread in Babylon and the ancient Near East, most popularly under King Hammurabi.[1] But every group in history had their own creation story, and many had similarities between them, such as chaos in the waters, a flood story, creation of man, talking snakes, etc. So the fact that the Jewish and Christian tradition has a creation story is far from unique.

What makes ours different is what it says.

Our creation story is beautiful.

The Hebrew Creation Story

The creation story I subscribe to, and I'm assuming you do as well, is the one found in the book of Genesis.

It is a beautiful poem. An origin story of guidance. A new way to think. So as you are reading through it over the next few pages, approach the text with fresh eyes. Try to understand the importance of the story in relation to the original audience.

In the beginning, God created the heavens and the earth. Now the earth was formless and empty, darkness was over the surface of the deep, and the Spirit of God was hovering over the waters.

And God said, "Let there be light," and there was light. God saw that the light was good, and he separated the light from the darkness. God called the light "day," and the darkness he called "night." And there was evening, and there was morning—the first day.

And God said, "Let there be a vault between the waters to separate water from water." So God made the vault and separated the water under the vault from the water above it. And it was so. God called the vault "sky." And there was evening, and there was morning—the second day.

And God said, "Let the water under the sky be gathered to one place, and let dry ground appear." And it was so. God called the dry ground "land," and the gathered waters he called "seas." And God saw that it was good.

Then God said, "Let the land produce vegetation: seed-bearing plants and trees on the land that bear fruit with seed in it, according to their various kinds." And it was so. The land produced vegetation: plants bearing seed according to their kinds and trees bearing fruit with seed in it according to their kinds. And God saw that it was good. And there was evening, and there was morning—the third day.

And God said, "Let there be lights in the vault of the sky to separate the day from the night, and let them serve as signs to mark sacred times, and days and years, and let them be lights in the vault of the sky to give light on the earth." And it was so. God made two great lights— the greater light to govern the day and the lesser light to govern the night. He also made the stars. God set them in the vault of the sky to give light on the earth, to govern the day and the night, and to separate light from darkness. And God saw that it was good. And there was evening, and there was morning—the fourth day.

And God said, "Let the water teem with living creatures, and let birds fly above the earth across the vault of the sky." So God created the great creatures of the sea and every living thing with which the water teems and that moves about in it, according to their kinds, and every winged bird according to its kind. And God saw that it was good. God blessed them and said, "Be fruitful and increase in number and fill the water in the seas, and let the birds increase on the earth." And there was evening, and there was morning—the fifth day.

And God said, "Let the land produce living creatures according to their kinds: the livestock, the creatures that move along the ground, the wild animals, each according to its kind." And it was so. God made the wild animals according to their kinds, the livestock according to their kinds, and all the creatures that move along the ground according to their kinds. And God saw that it was good.

Then God said, "Let us make mankind in our image, in our likeness, so that they may rule over the fish in the sea and the birds in the sky, over the livestock and all the wild animals, and over all the creatures that move along the ground." So God created mankind in his own image, in the image of God he created them; male and female he created them.

God blessed them and said to them, "Be fruitful and increase in number; fill the earth and subdue it. Rule over the fish in the sea and the birds in the sky and over every living creature that moves on the ground."

Then God said, "I give you every seed-bearing plant on the face of the whole earth and every tree that has fruit with seed in it. They will be yours for food. And to all the beasts of the earth and all the birds in the sky and all the creatures that move along the ground—everything that has the breath of life in it—I give every green plant for food." And it was so. God saw all that he had made, and it was very good. And there was evening, and there was morning—the sixth day.

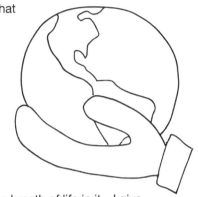

Genesis 1:1–31 NIV

First off, can we just acknowledge how hardcore it is that in our story, YHWH is hovering above the waters where these "chief gods"—Apsu and Tiamat—supposedly originated? And all he has to do is speak. It's a punch in the face to their neighbors.

God speaks and things are created. No resistance at all.

Light.

Sky.

Land.

Seas.

Plants.

Sun and moon.

Animals.

Man.

For three days God separated things, and the following three days he filled them.

After everything God created, he said, "It is good." We literally see this divine community of love receiving joy by creating things.

He created you and said you were good.

He created me and said I was good.

Our origin is based on goodness.

And our God has no rivals.

What are some things that you say are good?

Brownies are good.

Friendships are good.

There is a California burger company that I would say is *very* good.

So as the Hebrew Scriptures were being penned and organized while they were in exile, this is the story the Israelites were grasping on to. Their history was full of love and generosity and goodness, not violence and destruction like the others. Their story was different. So of course it endured. Of course they read this one and it meant something. It was in complete opposition to what they were being taught. They were seeing how to be optimistic in a pessimistic society.

In the words of author and professor Walter Brueggemann, "The text announces the deepest mystery: God wills and will have a faithful relation with earth. The text invites the listening community to celebrate that reality."[2]

To me, God is saying to us,

> All of this is good.
> You no longer have to work for me.
> I want to be in a relationship with you.
> I created everything for your benefit, not mine.

How mind-blowing is that? The prisoners of the Babylonian empire were now provided the ability to imagine an alternative reality that ran counter to the origin story of the empire itself. Incredible.

The first video game I played was *The Oregon Trail* in elementary school computer class. Our teachers claimed the game was educational, but all I remember is hunting and dying of dysentery, whatever that is. If your character successfully traveled from Missouri to Oregon, they were awarded points based on how many others survived and what possessions they had acquired along the way.

The cool thing about video games is how they often allow us to view life from a different perspective, just as the Hebrews were able to do.

And what's even cooler is that when God said, "Be fruitful and increase in number; fill the earth and subdue it,"[3] it meant Adam and Eve were now co-creators with God. They represented him on earth. Not only were they meant to protect Eden, but also to expand its boundaries to the ends of the earth, essentially filling the earth with the presence of God, to enjoy the world together.

This was the original plan.

And this is what God wants us to go back to.

Your view of the world and our role in it is based on understanding this point: to expand God's presence on earth.

Jesus as New Creation

Jesus had a cousin, John the Baptist, who would have been super weird according to today's standards. He spent his time in the wilderness, apart from everyone and everything, soaking in the presence of God and waiting for his time to come.

John had a serious responsibility: to usher in the Messiah.

When Mary, Jesus' mother, went to visit her cousin, Elizabeth, to share the news of her pregnancy, Elizabeth was also pregnant at the time. The story goes that when Mary walked into the room, John began to rejoice inside the stomach of Elizabeth.[4] He knew the presence of God even before he was born. So John's entire life was spent preparing for the announcement of the Messiah, his cousin, Jesus.

In Judaism, there was something called a *mikveh*.[5]

A mikveh was a ceremonial cleansing that was required before entering the presence of God inside the temple.

As much as the modern-day American church may talk against the Pharisees and the Law, the original intent behind every ritual was beautiful. They held God in such high respect. So a mikveh was meant to be an act of respect before going into the presence of God. But some people took the religiosity of it too far, and it inhibited access to God.

John the Baptist took a different approach.

He went straight to the Jordan River and began baptizing people, preparing them for the coming king, instead of approaching it from a traditional sense.[6]

You first need to realize how symbolic this was.

The Jordan River was where God reenacted the Red Sea crossing for the Hebrews.

It was the entrance into the Promised Land.

And John, by inviting people directly into the water instead of having them go through the mikveh ritual, was saying that they no longer needed the system because they could go straight to God themselves.

Every piece of this story was important.

Because of what John was doing, people began to question whether he himself was Christ, but John said, "I baptize you with water, but he who is mightier than I is coming, the strap of whose sandals I am not worthy to untie. He will baptize you with the Holy Spirit and fire."[7]

One day, Jesus came from Galilee to the Jordan River to be baptized by his cousin John. Even though it may seem like Jesus should be baptizing John, Jesus' baptism was necessary to fulfill his calling. This is how it went down:

"And when Jesus was baptized, immediately he went up from the water, and behold, the heavens were opened to him, and he saw the Spirit of God descending like a dove and coming to rest on him; and behold, a voice from heaven said, 'This is my beloved Son, with whom I am well pleased.'"[8]

Sound familiar at all?

Think about Genesis 1, our creation story.

Jesus enters the water, which is chaos, and when he comes out, a divine voice speaks, saying, "This is my beloved Son."

Every Jewish reader is going to understand the importance of this moment. This symbolizes a completely new creation. A new Adam. Life. The world used to be unknown, chaotic, and that's where the new creation comes into play. Things are different now.

And how was Jesus going to baptize you? With the Holy Spirit and fire.

In Isaiah 40–55, we see how closely connected the outpouring of the Holy Spirit is to new creation.

It's all about new creation.

When you begin a relationship with Jesus, you are taking on this new creation so that when God the Father looks at you, he sees the transformation of his Son, Jesus, inside of you.

The Final New Creation

The more I study the Bible, the more I realize how warped many views of Scripture actually are, especially when it comes to the end times and where we are heading. People will make blanket statements about the book of Revelation and how terrible things are about to be and how angry God is.

We can often share hope with the hopeless and yet remain hopeless ourselves.

The Bible shows us that the world was created with peace and harmony and ends with peace and harmony, not violence.

We need to read the whole story, from front to back.

The last scene from the book of Revelation ends with New Creation, a merging of heaven and earth. It's not a story about how we go to heaven when we die and have golden castles in the clouds for eternity.

That's completely false.

The Bible message has always been and will always be about the kingdom of God on earth as it is in heaven. It's about putting things right, here, in the present and the future material world.

God didn't create all of this goodness and beauty just to blow it up one day and destroy his creation. No, he will be faithful and redeem what he started, transforming the world back to the original plan of Eden spread across the land.[9]

N. T. Wright writes in his book *Simply Good News,*

> The point is that the meaning of the good news changes radically depending on whether you think it means, "Here's how you leave this universe and go somewhere else called heaven," or whether you think it means, "Here's how God is remaking the entire creation and offering you a new bodily life within that." If we are promised new heaven and new earth, a whole new universe in which God's space and our space are brought together once and for all—and that's what the New Testament writers say again and again—then the good news is news about, and news *for*, the whole of creation, not just a few humans who get the magic password that lets them off the hook into heaven after all.[10]

New creation is for everyone.

If they want it.

NEW CREATION

- IS FOR -

EVERYONE

In the book of Philippians, Paul is writing to the church there and explains how our citizenship is in heaven.[11] I understand how this may be confusing, considering what I've been saying. Check this out. Rome was very over-crowded at the time, everyone was living in the big city, so there was no peace and quiet, no suburban life to get away to.

When the Roman soldiers came back from war, there was essentially no room for them in the city anymore, so the Roman government created colonies all over North-ern Greece for these Roman soldiers to go to. Their role wasn't to go back to Rome but to spread the Roman way of life among these new colonies.

So when Paul is saying that their citizenship is in heaven, sure it is, but that's not where they are going to float off to eventually. They were to focus on their surroundings.

To take it even further, the word *apostle* was actually the title of people in the Roman government whose job was to go into the newly conquered cities and be culture carriers. Their role was to bring the culture of Rome into new places.

So when Jesus commissions the apostles to go out into all the world and spread the Good News, he's alluding to the task of bringing a kingdom culture into every new space, every new field they went into. Their role was to bring the heavenly way of life to the new colony they lived in, whether that was in Philippi or New York City or Madagascar.

No matter where we are, the final new creation is coming. And our role has already been enacted. We are co-creators with God, active agents in history welcoming the oncoming kingdom, expanding the edges of Eden in our day-to-day lives, in our communities, around the world.

We were made in the image of God.

We represent him.

He wants to use us to get things back on track.

All he wants is for his people to say, "Yes, use me, Lord."

There is a phrase many ancient Jewish rabbis used: *tikkun olam*.[12]

Tikkun can be translated as "repair."

To fix.

To improve.

To build upon.

To create.

Olam means "the world."

So *tikkun olam* has to do with any activity that improves the world around us, creating something new, something better than the way we found it.

In Jewish thought, the world was good at its core, but God left room for us to work it, to co-create together.

How do we live this out?

One day at a time in simple acts of kindness and obedience.

Building a family that glorifies God.
Standing up for the hurting and marginalized.
Feeding the hungry.
Lending an ear.
Making your friends laugh.
Being a person of peace.
Being kind.
Buying your neighbor a cup of coffee.
Bringing hope to the hopeless, the real way.

Your Creation Story

Show me the creation story you believe—the one from our Bible or one from Babylon or elsewhere—and I'll tell you what kind of life you're living.

Is it about scarcity and violence?

Or is it about joy and generosity and abundance and diversity?

One viewpoint leads to optimism while the other leads to seeing the world as falling apart.

Genesis shows us how creative and diverse God's love is.

He put land here.
And sky up there.
And flowers in your garden.
And trees in your backyard.

All of it to enjoy because the differences make life awesome.

The first time my wife jumped in a pile of snow, it was full of dirt and ice. A peculiar thud sounded.

I wouldn't have let it happen had I known her intentions, but she had opened the door and took a run for it. I knew that a pile of snow on the side of a parking lot is different from untouched snow in a field. But to her, it was all snow and it was all new and it was all beautiful. To me, it was just . . . snow. I grew up with it and had become numb to the beauty.

So we built a snowman named Tommy.

He was a proper snowman with coal for eyes, a carrot nose, and a plaid scarf. Our friends Ethan and Allie supported us in our endeavors, rolling gigantic snowballs that required multiple people to lift them on top of each other and to make sure Tommy's aesthetic was top of the line.

How many moments do we miss out on by becoming numb to the beauty? How many snowmen from Tommy's extended family are never built because we have lost the joy of creation?

I don't want to be that person anymore.

The Bible keeps going back to the understanding that it's good to be here, it's good to be human, let's make a new world together and restore all that was lost. That's the through line.

People need to be told what's possible, not how terrible a person they are.

We live in a wonderful world. God gave this creation to us as a gift. How we view life depicts how we will love others.

And God said it was all good.

CHAPTER 4

Shabbat

I THREW UP a lot as a kid.

There were certain smells and environments that just overwhelmed and brought out the worst in me. Or, rather, brought *up* the worst in me.

I would nervously watch the clock on the wall at school ticking closer and closer to lunchtime. It was overwhelming because, well, the cafeteria happened to be my routine "mess" hall. It got to the point where the school made me eat in the classroom instead of the cafeteria with everybody else.

My teacher would ask the entire class, "Does anyone want to volunteer to eat with Zach today?"

How embarrassing.

But I get it; the school caught on, and they were not about that clean-up life. Looking back, it was probably a good thing. If I hadn't been confined to lonely classroom lunches, I might not have met my friend Dave.

Dave was new in town. He didn't know me. I didn't know him. On the first day of fourth grade, our teacher asked that dreaded question and looked for somebody who would volunteer to eat with me. Since Dave didn't know anybody, I'm guessing he thought, *What the heck. I'll eat with the kid.*

Bold move, Dave. Bold move.

That was day one of a friendship I still appreciate. Back then, it benefited Dave because he was new, and it benefited me because I needed someone to help me from the social suicide of being the lone lunch boy.

The situation got a bit better in middle school. My body started handling the stress better; I no longer had teachers asking for volunteers to eat with me. Life was good. I discovered the morning miracle of Pepcid AC and typically had a two-minute window before eureka.

Nonetheless, although things were better, the problem wasn't completely gone. One of the worst experiences happened on a trip to Canada with my church youth group. It was so bad that it's become one of my highlight stories now that I'm an adult. Isn't it weird how that works?

In any case, we were headed to a campground to serve around the property and help the people. I'm not sure if child labor laws would allow things like that these days, but times change and we learn from our experiences.

If you remember, young Zach couldn't handle certain smells and environments. Now, I am not trying to be mean, but there was a kid on the trip who clearly didn't like to wash his hair. Maybe he was allergic to shampoo, I don't know. But that hair looked like it was coated in wax. Basically, it was a butter sculpture pompadour. You could surf on it.

And my stomach turned at every glance.

Pair the hair with the DJ Tiësto playing in my left earbud from my friend's Discman, and it was not a good combo. With every bass hit, my stomach responded. With every beat drop, so did my confidence in being able to withstand it all. I have the wax sculpture in front of me while listening to club music on a bus jam-packed full of antsy teenagers.

I was done for.

It felt like a *Mission: Impossible* scene to get to that bus bathroom. I thought, *Where was my two-minute warning?* Inevitably, I did not make it. And the worst part about it is that everybody had to deal with the smell of my failure for the next eight hours. I was *that* kid. Instantly public enemy number one.

Life was very frustrating because of my vomiting problem. It stuck with me from elementary school through middle school and further. I really had no idea why this happened to me or what the problem was. As time went on and I got older, I found out my dad and grandma dealt with the same issue in their early childhood years.

The culprit? Anxiety.

People everywhere around the world feel anxious in some capacity. But it is so interesting that anxiety can begin at such a young age. How can a fourth grader be anxious about life?

It's as if it is ingrained into our nervous system. And it continues into our adult life unless we do something about it. At a certain point, we must rewrite the narrative.

Rewriting that narrative is something I still struggle to do. Being surrounded by hustle culture and the no-days-off mindset has always seemed normal, a part of the culture I lived in.

It's all go, go, go.

Many of us think we are defined by our productivity. And if we can't keep up the pace, we feel as though we are falling behind, and we push even harder.

How messed up is that?

Doesn't God say something about rest? Doesn't he actually command it in his Word?

I've been an entrepreneur my entire adult life. And for a long time, side hustles were my everything. I would brag about how I didn't take a day off for six years, including holidays. I didn't go on a proper vacation for a decade. I would work twelve to sixteen hours per day, seven days a week. And you know what it did for me?

It made me sick and anxious.

Can you relate to any of the following?

I'm afraid of failing.
I'm afraid of letting people down.
I'm afraid of not being able to take care of my family.
I struggle with my worth.
I feel like I always need to prove something.
I feel like I'm one day away from losing it all.
I think I can control outcomes.
I question what all of this is about.
I question my calling.
I wonder why we are here.
I compare myself with others.
I need to be the last one standing.
I struggle with imposter syndrome.
I get impatient when things are going too slowly.
I feel the need to produce, produce, produce.

The list could go on and on. I think about that a lot. I also think about what freedom would look like, don't you? What if we operated and lived life against the norm? What if we finally made the time to rewrite our story—our narrative? What if we lived a life where we were at peace, where creativity flowed, where we could take a step back and breathe a little bit?

Escaping the hustle culture allows us to open our eyes to the goodness that God created all around us. We can finally be human *beings* instead of human *doings*. We can be who God intended us to be.

Rest as Countercultural

Have you ever been horseback riding? Not at a fair or carnival, but for real, riding a horse in the back country? It's pretty wild. When I was on a trip in the mountains, a surprise offer to go horseback riding made its way to my doorstep.

We woke up that day and it was absolutely pouring rain. This should have been a sign for how the day was going to go, as I think God was saying, "Stay home!" But we went anyway after putting on an unnecessary number of layers to protect us from the elements. I know I'm from Minnesota, but quite frankly, I don't think anybody likes being cold and wet at the same time.

Upon arriving for our ride, we had two options: hang out inside where it was warm and dry while the guides set up our horses, or hang out in the rain. Simple choice, if you ask me. However, the cabin smelled like horse droppings. It was a lose-lose situation, and I was ready to take it all in. No bad vibes were going to impact my day.

We eventually filed into the stable to meet our horses before riding out. Each one was named something strange, like Trixie, Lightning, Spunk, etc.

I guess I'm not really sure what a normal horse name would be.

Jordan?

Tim?

Meredith?

Maybe those are weirder than Lightning and Trixie.

My horse was named Popcorn.

"That's an odd name for a horse," I said.

"Oh, that's because she *pops* every once in a while," the guide responded, then chuckled.

"What do you mean, 'Pops every once in a while'?!"

No answer.

My nerves kicked in. I'm all about being adventurous, but I had no idea what I was doing on a horse, and my safety was now in question.

Our guide opened the gate and we all began to trot out into the field at a slow pace, getting comfortable having a beast underneath each of us.

This is simple, I thought. *No problems here.* That is, until the leader began to move faster, heading straight for the base of the mountain and disappearing into the woods. We were flying at this point.

I was bouncing up and down, my legs going in directions I've never felt before, and I had to remove my glasses because the rain was still dumping.

Everyone looked like a real cowboy. Except for me. I'm sure I looked like a Raggedy Ann doll, with a smile plastered on my face, not sure if it was out of excitement or having no idea what was going on.

As we worked our way along the trails, heading up the mountain, we came to a fork in the trail. I was in the middle of the pack, and everyone in front of me went right at the fork, but Popcorn had her own plans and called an audible. To the left we go!

She took off, leaving the horses behind us in her dust. Yes, this is what the guide meant when she said that Popcorn "pops" every once in a while.

She didn't care where the rest were going. She had her own plans, and I was officially a mountaineer, out on my own. But you know what? Something happened inside me and I just kept kicking her sides to go faster. Nothing could stop us. We were free.

Sometimes it's important to go against the norm and call an audible, just as Popcorn did. When everyone is going right, it's okay to go left. A lot of the time that's where true freedom is, especially in our culture today.

Obeying the sabbath is commanded of the Israelites two different times in Scripture, but it is probably the most overlooked commandment to the majority of Gentiles today. We tend to claim, "I'm always living in a state of rest," but are we really? Maybe that's just an excuse for not slowing down as we should.

The first instance where we see the Sabbath as a command is when Moses is given the Ten Commandments in the book of Exodus.[1] Remember, the Israelites had just been in slavery for the last four hundred years, and all they knew how to do was work for Pharaoh.

They were in a system of oppression that only valued them based on how much they could produce. It was all about the bricks.

And now God is changing things up on them. His suggestions were completely countercultural.[2]

But a slave mentality doesn't disappear overnight, so God provided the Israelites with a handbook of rules to follow, bringing them closer to holiness and the original intent for relationship with God.

God introduces the Ten Commandments by saying, "I am the LORD your God, who brought you out of the land of Egypt, out of the house of slavery,"[3] and keeping the sabbath is the fourth commandment.

> Remember the Sabbath day, to keep it holy. Six days you shall labor, and do all your work, but the seventh day is a Sabbath to the LORD your God. On it you shall not do any work, you or your son, or your daughter, your male servant, or your female servant, or your livestock, or the sojourner who is within your gates. For in six days the LORD made heaven and earth, the sea, and all that is in them, and rested on the seventh day. Therefore the LORD blessed the Sabbath day and made it holy.
>
> Exodus 20:8–11

They were supposed to rest because God rested. Simple and plain.

Karl Barth observed that if God created humanity on the sixth day and the sabbath on the seventh day, that means the first thing their existence is predicated on is rest and relationship with the Creator. It's the first event they experienced! And now God was commanding them to participate in it weekly![4]

But that got lost somewhere along the way.

We might not be required to practice the sabbath in the same way today, but I truly believe there is so much wisdom in taking time to rest and remember that Jesus is Lord.

Restlessness is killing us, and we need to slow down for a bit.

So if that means you take one day every week to shut off the outside world, to spend time with friends and family, to read, to eat good food, to nap, do it.

If it helps you become more aware of God's presence so you can see God's goodness in your life, do it.

If it helps you be present, do it.

If it helps you grow closer to Jesus, do it.

Besides, everyone loves a good reason to celebrate.

CHAPTER 5

It's a Celebration

I WORKED in the hospitality industry for twelve years.

I started off serving tables poolside at a local country club in order to pull knowledge by being in proximity to some of the area's wealthiest people. After a few years, I worked my way up in the industry. I managed restaurants and eventually even helped open one.

I have so much respect for every person in the industry because I know how much of a grind it can be. Their jobs are literally to make people smile, whether or not the customer woke up on the right side of the bed.

And oftentimes, they didn't.

The most fulfilling job I had in the service industry was at a restaurant in Minneapolis called Spoon and Stable. It was truly an honor to be a part of their team. I think a lot of it had to do with the respect we all had for chef/owner, Gavin Kaysen, who is literally one of the most incredible chefs in the world.

Kaysen is not only a world-renowned chef, he was also president of Team USA at a cooking competition in France called Bocuse d'Or, which is basically the Olympics of cooking. And with his lead as vice president in 2017, the U.S. took home the gold medal, a feat never accomplished before. The U.S. had placed on the leaderboard only one time before, in 2015, when he was the competing chef.

Chef Kaysen is a master of his craft.

He's a master at making people feel special.

Hospitality is in this man's blood.

Working in his restaurants inspires employees to greatness, and being plugged in inspires them to look at every person, every moment, as an opportunity to impact a person's life in a meaningful way. Each worker can control the experience to either provide just another dinner or instill a memory that will last a lifetime.

As employees of Chef Kaysen, we wanted to make sure every single person felt like there was nobody else in the room. Our undivided attention was on them and their experience. Every detail was attended to, beginning the moment the guest walked in the door. And if they were there for a special occasion—whether an anniversary, a birthday, a promotion, anything worth celebrating—it was even better, kind of like a challenge to make them feel all the feels.

One fun way of making the moment memorable was by bringing a gigantic cone of cotton candy out to the guest.

You know how most places give you a sundae?

Well, we gave them a cloud of cotton candy the size of two of their heads.

Or I guess one, if they had a big head.

I'm convinced that you cannot have a bad day if you are handed a large cotton candy sculpture.

Chef Kaysen played a major part in developing my love for people and my passion for making others feel special around the table.

On my last day working at Spoon and Stable, the pastry chef allowed me to

spin a stick of cotton candy myself. I lit up. Joy was flowing out of me. Because even though it was bittersweet to be leaving the business, I remembered that you can't have a bad day when you're given cotton candy. And boy was that correct.

I want to remember those moments and lessons for the rest of my life.

When was the last time you had a chance to celebrate life? Has it been a while? For some of us, it may have been years ago. For others, it may have been yesterday.

I think God loves it when we celebrate. He loves it when joy contagiously overflows us. And I think that happens most often when we are content with our current situation, when we enjoy those around us, and when we can ac-knowledge that everything is a gift from God.

"I Command You to Feast!"

The state of Minnesota is best known for having a whole bunch of lakes, Scandinavian traditions, and the world-famous Minnesota State Fair.

I'm not sure if that last one's true, but the fair sure feels like it's world famous to me. It's basically a twelve-day celebration of culture, the good and the bad entwined together.

I think the one thing that charges me up more than any-thing else is getting people to experience new things, whether it's something adventurous or a unique food.

The Minnesota State Fair is the perfect culmination of both.

Now that I am older, a lot of my friends live in different states, and we love visiting each other to see what life is like in their neck of the woods. When people talk about visiting Minnesota, I suggest they come at the end of Au-gust in order to experience the fair.

What makes our fair unique is that it's one of the biggest in the country, and people travel from all over just to experi-ence it—like, more than a million people every day. The food is great, but eating is not all you can do.

There are rides, concerts, people-watching, shows, art exhibits, nature exhibits, the whole deal. They even carve people out of butter in a refrigerated glass box. It's wild. And I love every second of it.

If you live in Minnesota, there's a fifty-fifty chance you actually enjoy going. And that 50 percent might go once a year or maybe every other year. But I'm not like most people. I go a minimum of three times each year, typically more.

With friends visiting from out of town, I become a tour guide. We don't mess around, though. We need to keep it moving. My friend Jesse says, "When you go to the fair with Zach, you might not wake up the next day, but if you do, your ankles will be killing you."

Like I said, we keep it moving.

The Minnesota State Fair is a celebration of life. And we live it well.

All throughout the Bible we see God telling his people to celebrate. He actually commands them to throw these huge feasts throughout the year as a time to refocus, recenter, and remember that all provision comes from God.

Joseph Pieper said, "The happiness of being created, the existential goodness of things, the participation in the life of God, the overcoming of death—all the occasions of the great traditional festivals are pure gift."[1]

Every feast was about the gift of being alive.

And God wanted his people to party.

In the Babylonian creation story we looked at earlier, humans were created to work for the gods and give them food offerings to meet their needs.

At the end of Genesis 1, God gives Adam and Eve food to please them, not the other way around.

He completely rewrote the narrative they were being taught by their surrounding culture.

We think we know how to feast, but God actually taught the Israelites how to feast in the Bible. He made sure they celebrated life seven times throughout the year, in addition to the weekly Sabbath rest. These feasts were like an extended version of the Sabbath, pointing the people to the forever Sabbath rest of the future.

In Leviticus 23, God breaks down each festival in detail.

He said they were holy.

They were a time to worship him.

And they were a foreshadowing of the coming Messiah who would redeem the world, inviting all people into the kingdom.

The first four feasts were in the spring, while the other three were in the fall, reminding the Israelites of God's provision during harvest seasons, and how even when they rest in him, God will still provide.

Spring Feasts

Passover was the first feast, a meal for everyone to enjoy. It was a time for the Israelites to remember when the Spirit of the Lord "passed over" their homes in Egypt and saved their firstborn children. From a larger perspective,

Passover is all about the redemption of sin. The Last Supper was actually a Passover meal.

The next day began a seven-day festival called the **Feast of Unleavened Bread**, when the Israelites had to remove yeast from their diet but could indulge in anything else. To the Israelites, this represented their exodus out of Egypt, leaving everything behind. In the New Testament, yeast often represented evil; this feast encourages us today to leave our old self behind.

Shortly after was the **Feast of Firstfruits**, on the Sabbath after the harvest began. The Israelites would bring the first portion of their harvest as an offering to God in gratitude for the provision ahead during harvest season.

The final spring festival was the **Feast of Weeks**, or **Pentecost**, as many call it. This took place fifty days after the Feast of Firstfruits, or seven Sabbaths after the Feast of Unleavened Bread. This feast was an extra Sabbath, like a jubilee Sabbath—another time to thank God for all his provision during the harvest.

Are you seeing a pattern here?

God loves it when we celebrate. And he actually considers our gratitude to be an act of worship.

Fall Feasts

The final three feasts take place during a one-month span. It was party after party after party. In the Jewish tradition, they called this trifecta of parties the Days of Awe and Wonder.

First was the **Feast of Trumpets**, a one-day event that marked the end of the harvest season and the beginning of a time of sacredness. The Israelites would just blow trumpets all day and celebrate life. From a Christian perspective, this represents the second coming of Jesus, which is said to take place at the sounding of the trumpet blast.

Nine days later, the Israelites were commanded to celebrate the **Day of Atonement**. This was a day when the high priest went into the Holy of Holies and made an offering on behalf of all the sins of Israel. Every year offered a fresh start, a sinless state.

Finally, five days later, the feast schedule wrapped up with another seven-day festival called the **Feast of Tabernacles**, when the Israelites would relive the wilderness wanderings by sleeping in huts outside their homes. Every day was a party. For seven days. And it was a foreshadowing of Jesus one day "tabernacling" again with us, with every nation, tribe, and tongue, here on earth, forever.

Feast after feast.
After feast.
After feast.
After feast after feast.
After feast.

God loves a good celebration. He loves making his people smile.

To take it one step further, in Deuteronomy 14, he gets extravagant with his commands. He says to bring the tithe of their harvest to Jerusalem to consume it and learn to fear the Lord always. And if they couldn't bring all of their tithe on the journey, "Then you shall turn it into money and bind up the money in your hand and go to the place that the Lord your God chooses and spend the money for whatever you desire—oxen or sheep or wine or strong drink, whatever your appetite craves. And you shall eat there before the Lord your God and rejoice, you and your household."[2]

God literally commands them to take 10 percent of their harvest and turn it into a party. Think about that for a second. Say you make $40,000 in a year. God was saying to take $4,000 of that and celebrate, throw a party, eat good food, drink good wine, laugh, dance, enjoy life to the fullest.

This was *commanded*! They didn't have a choice!

Feasting is one of the most consistent things throughout Scripture, so how can we be stuck in the mindset that things were getting worse?

God could have used the DMV or jail to describe life.

But he didn't.

He used feast, feast, party, dinner, wedding, celebration, supper, feast.

God is joyful. God is loving. God cares about your happiness and well-being far more than you ever could. I think that gets lost inside religion a lot of the time. But God does want us to celebrate. He created us to enjoy life—not be afraid and sulk in a doom and gloom mentality.

Jesus Came Eating and Drinking

In Jewish tradition, the Messiah was expected to come in glory and honor, with angel armies at his sides, ready to take over.

But Jesus arrived as a servant, coming to seek and save the lost.

Huh? That's quite different from what was expected.

And what did he do when he got here?

He ate and drank with people.

So much so that people considered him to be a glutton and drunkard, aka someone who eats and drinks too much.[3]

Jesus' version of evangelism was hospitality.[4] It was a way to demonstrate that he accepted those whom others despised. C. T. McMahan wrote about Jesus' table practice in the book of Luke, concluding:

> Of all the means by which Jesus could have chosen to be remembered, he chose to be remembered by a meal. What he considered memorable and characteristic of his ministry was his table-fellowship. The meal, one of humankind's most basic and common practices, was transformed by

Jesus into an occasion of divine encounter. It was in the
sharing of food and drink that he invited his companions
to share in the grace of God. The quintessence of Jesus'
redemptive mission was revealed in his eating with sinners,
repentant and unrepentant alike.[5]

His mission was revealed in his eating with sinners.

The table was a way to turn strangers into friends and to
invite everybody into the kingdom lifestyle. It was practical, not mystical.

Jesus was breaking all types of social taboos. A meal represented friendship and community and acceptance. Jesus
was saying that *all* are welcome into the kingdom now.

And it began with one bite.

One conversation.

By listening to what others were going through.

And actually being there for them.

This was a revolutionary way of thinking. That you could
actually worship God through good food, wine, celebration, and not only that, but people would convert their lives
through the process.

Jesus never taught about the fear of being left behind or
told us to sit in our misery.

Instead, his stories showed abundance and generosity
and joy and celebrating and love and welcoming of all and
laughter and great food and gratitude.

Story after story.

Parable after parable.

The message was always the same.

I'm often confused about how this can be missed.

Jesus' first public miracle was at a wedding.[6] These parties weren't just a few hours of celebration; they went all night long, and many of them spanned multiple days. Nonstop.

I've been to a lot of weddings, but never a wedding like this one.

At this particular wedding in Cana, the wine began to diminish, and the hosts tapped into the reserves, but people just kept on drinking. Jesus was at this wedding, and so was his mother, Mary, who knew how embarrassing it would have been for the hosts to run out of wine. The neighbors would have talked negatively behind the hosts' backs for weeks to come.

Jesus noticed there were six pots of water used for ritual purification on the property. These were massive pots; you would use them to purify your hands before eating, or your entire body before entering the temple.

These pots were important. And so was the water in them.

One time—a time I wasn't really chasing after my faith—my friend Heather and I went to visit our other friend at his church. He was playing music and we thought it would be a fun surprise. In this specific church, they had a basin of holy water in the foyer to dip your finger in and mark a cross on your forehead.

I'm not going to lie, Heather was a little wild for doing this: She dipped her fingers in the water and pretended to sneeze on me, spraying the water on my face.

I was mortified.

Every eye in the room was glaring at us for the rest of the service. How embarrassing.

So Jesus was looking at these pots of water and told the waitstaff to fill the large jars with water and then fill up their jugs from there. The servants' jugs were filled with the best wine anybody in the region had tasted. The party was saved, along with the hosts' image. Jesus turned the party up a notch.

Remember, this was his first public miracle. How random is that?

In Luke 15, Jesus is eating dinner at Levi's house with a bunch of bad dudes. Like, the worst of the worst.

And outside the party were the Pharisees and teachers of the Law. These guys were zealous for the Lord and lived in fear of him—rightfully so, considering they didn't want to go back into exile. But their religion got in the way of what God was really trying to do.

So Jesus was eating with these guys who the Pharisees thought were despicable, and who had, in reality, been bringing oppression to the Jewish people for years. It didn't make sense to them for the so-called Messiah to be dining amongst them.

This small act was also revolutionary and went against all social standards. To eat with someone meant they were accepted to the feast just as they were.

So of course the Pharisees started saying mean things about Jesus and questioning his actions. That makes sense!

To explain his actions, Jesus shares a parable in the form of three stories, all showing the same thing.

Something is lost,

It is then found,

And a party follows.

The first is about a shepherd who has a hundred sheep. Right out of the gate, Jesus is being funny here because shepherding was a dirty job, and none of the Pharisees would ever imagine taking on that task. Jesus tells of one sheep that goes missing and how the shepherd leaves the other ninety-nine behind to find the one.

After finding the runaway sheep, the shepherd returns to the community and they throw a party over this one found sheep. We don't even know what happened to the other sheep. They could still be in the woods. What we do know is that this shepherd left everything behind to bring it back; the sheep itself did nothing except run away.

Have you ever lost something important to you? How did that make you feel? The worst, right? You know exactly what Jesus is talking about here—with the joy that comes from recovering something precious.

Jesus then moves on to tell the story of a woman who had ten coins but lost one of them. She searched and searched and searched until one day she found the lost coin and she threw a party. Again, the coin didn't do anything to be found, just as the sheep did not. But both the woman and the shepherd threw a party.

The third parable Jesus shares is about two sons. One of them asks his father for his share of the inheritance. We can often skip over this part of the story without really thinking about it, but to ask for an inheritance early meant the son was saying, "Dad, you are dead to me. Sell part of your land and give me what is mine." Yikes.

The father in that moment is supposed to slap the son across his face. This was absolutely uncalled for! At most, the son could just leave the family business and run away, but never would he ask for his inheritance early. And never would the father actually grant his request.

But this father does.

The son takes his inheritance to a faraway land and blows it all. Now he's in trouble. Broke as can be, he gets a job working on a farm feeding the pigs, covered in mud and feces. About as nasty as you can get.

He had enough. The prodigal son says to himself, "I remember my father had servants. Maybe I could go back to the house, work for him to make a living, and reestablish our family relationship."

As the boy returned to his home city with his head down, covered in shame, he was ready to beg for a second chance. But what we see is something much different.

The father sees the son from a distance and begins to run toward him. During this time in society, a father never would have run, and he definitely wouldn't have welcomed his son back without extreme ramifications.

But this father was different.

He ran so quickly, making a fool of himself, he hugged his boy, telling the slaves to put the finest robe on him, the finest shoes on his feet, and to throw the biggest party.

His son who was lost was now found. Their relationship was mended. And the entire village came together to celebrate this moment.

The shepherd, the woman, and the father all throw a party to celebrate the return of that which was lost. And this is exactly what happens in heaven when one person who was lost is found.

Jesus is saying that everyone is invited to the party, even the worst of the worst.

He invites you and me.

Not to sit outside and scoff at the unrighteous being saved, but to approach every situation with grace and invite others inside with us. Because in these stories, the sheep, the coin, and the son didn't do anything to be found. They all had still belonged the entire time.

Jesus was preaching joy and generosity and love and goodness. He wasn't preaching about all of the bad things that were happening in the world. He was saying that the kingdom was now here.

And things in the kingdom are way, way different.

We need to be celebrating how *we* have been found.

Not wondering if we are good enough to enjoy it. No, we have already been accepted. Once you acknowledge that there isn't anything you can do to make God love you more, you can live from a place of joy and begin to share life with those around you.

Now you can really live.

In the Old Testament, the prophet Isaiah describes a gigantic feast in the future, known as the Messianic Banquet.

> On this mountain the Lord of hosts will make for all peoples
>   a feast of rich food, a feast of well-aged wine,
>   of rich food full of marrow, of aged wine well refined.
> And he will swallow up on this mountain
>   the covering that is cast over all peoples,
>   the veil that is spread over all nations.
>   He will swallow up death forever;
> and the Lord God will wipe away tears from all faces,
>   and the reproach of his people he will take away from all
>   the earth,
> for the Lord has spoken.
>
> Isaiah 25:6–8

Feast.
Food.
Wine.
All people.
All nations.
All faces.
All the earth.

Verse after verse
throughout the
Bible is all about
a coming feast
and the celebration
of our Messiah, Jesus Christ.

In the future, death will be eliminated, and the world will be returned to its original plan, as a place for all of us to enjoy the presence of God for all eternity.

Jesus is hosting the party, and we are welcome to join.

Change the World

Jesus was often criticized when he spoke of abundance and celebration. The religious leaders just expected him to be different. He wasn't really lining up with their preconceived ideas about what the Messiah would be like.

He was saying that the kingdom was here.

Everyone was invited.

Everyone was welcome.

You no longer needed to sulk in your misery or self-righteousness.

Hope was alive and well.

And could be attained through a relationship with Jesus.

We have the ability to be surrounded by God's presence today; we don't need to wait for a time in the future. New creation always involves feasting. So we can celebrate now in the abundance, joy, peace, love, and fellowship that comes with being a believer. And we can keep our eyes on the future party that's still to come, where all of creation will be renewed.

For now, we can follow Jesus' model and learn how to celebrate life instead of being bummed out all the time. A lot of people always find something to complain about. Don't be one of them. Nobody will want what you have. You can quote Bible verses all day, but if you have a crap creation story, it doesn't matter. Great meals are crafted with great ingredients.

And I believe the key to changing the world is by doing it one meal at a time.

Instead of making it weird, let's meet people where they are and enjoy a cheeseburger together.

Maybe you'll have a moment to share about what God is doing in your life.

Or maybe you won't.

Maybe that meal will be just a breath of fresh air, a time when you don't have to look for a way to evangelize and instead can enjoy your time with someone who might see things differently. So often we project our insecurities on others who don't think the same way we do, instead of being confident in who we were created to be.

I believe the best way to love others is at the table.

Sometimes you'll get to share your faith.

But other times you may just need to lend an ear and enjoy a great glass of wine.

And there's no shame in that.

CHAPTER 6

He's Way Funnier in Real Life

I DIDN'T MEAN TO GOOGLE what Jesus looked like, it just kind of happened.

Truly I was trying to find out if Jesus had specifically said something, because, you know, I like to fact-check statements people make on social media. Social media has created a whole bunch of preachers who shouldn't be preachers, and honestly, I don't trust a lot of them. So I fact-check.

I typed in "Did Jesus ever . . ." when Google began to guess which direction my question was going.

. . . get married?

. . . baptize anyone?

. . . cry?

. . . laugh or smile?

Wait.

What do you mean, did Jesus ever laugh or smile? What a funny question. Of course he did! Or do people not agree with that? Is that why Google suggested it? Because so many people have asked?

So I did it. I Googled "What did Jesus look like?"

I literally laughed out loud.

You're kidding me.

Every single picture of Jesus was straight-faced. Serious. Maybe a hint of sadness, but aside from that, emotionless. And light skin, a six pack, and European features—but that's an entirely different topic we'll get into another time. I guess I just assumed we had gotten over that old-school view of him. I mean, we are in the twenty-first century now and have been studying him for 2,000 years. Anyway, on this particular day, I was thinking more about his joy. And laughter. And smile.

All throughout the Bible, Jesus is described as joyful.[1]

But art and society display him as somber and judgmental.

A monastery in the Sinai Peninsula—St. Catherine's Monastery—houses one of the oldest paintings of Jesus. The artist was intentional with this painting of Jesus in order to show two aspects of Christ at once. He is holding a book with a cross on it in one arm and making the sign of blessing with his other hand. His eyes are really what got me, though. It looked to me like one eye is squinted with judgment while the other is kind with forgiveness.

Your view of Jesus' personality influences your relationship with him more than almost anything else. It's all about which eye you look into. If you think he is mad at you, your relationship will be based on fear. If you think he is disappointed, the same thing.

And there's nothing worse than someone saying, "I'm not mad, I'm just disappointed."

Gag me.

I have always thought of Jesus as fun-loving and joyful. Like, he smiled way more than anyone else did. I don't know where that mindset came from, but it stuck with me. Did you know that God actually knows what makes you smile better than you do?[2] How cool is that!

For years I believed that one of the best ways to show the love of Christ was through a smile. I created a clothing line around the idea. I wrote songs about it. I even started a movement of sorts in college called the "Pick Your Smile Up" movement.

It was based on a line in one of my old songs that said,

> With two thumbs to the sky,
> Bright whites shining wide,
> Happy people on the rise,
> It's time to point your smiles to me,
> Pick your smiles up.

The phrase clicked and kind of became my motto for a long time. I'd say it still is, I just don't have it branded on anything anymore.

Thrift-Store Jesus

I fell away from God for a while in college, even though I went to a Christian university. It's strange how that can happen—being surrounded by people who are furthering their faith but you're searching for something different. I often say it was the darkness inside of me that was at war with the light inside of them. The more I think about it, that might just be an excuse.

I wanted something practical.

I wanted something real.

I wanted to see Jesus lived out in day-to-day life, not some fake ideology that had no influence on our actions.

I guess I just expected people to be more loving and less judgmental and kind and joyful and . . . smiley?

My friends David and Peter had this house close by where we would hang out from time to time. They were really cool, trendy guys, and I liked having conversations with them. We all did.

They had a wall in their house that was covered in paintings of Jesus they found at local thrift stores.

And every one of them made me depressed.

I could be sitting in the kitchen or the dining room or the living room and Jesus was always staring at me. I'm not sure if it's because I felt convicted for not really chasing after my faith or what, but Jesus did not look happy with me.

Honestly, it made me so nervous I would make excuses for all of us to hang out on the front stoop. I didn't want to go inside and deal with my internal struggle, seeing disappointment in his eyes.

Have you ever felt that way when looking at a picture of Jesus?

Maybe the church you grew up in had a hallway lined with pictures of Jesus and his facial expression is ingrained in your memory.

How strange is that? Think of how those images impacted your view of him. And how different it would have been if you saw Jesus laughing and full of smiles.

Brazilian Jesus

One of my best friends is the world-renowned artist Tiago Magro.

Tiago loves the church and does an incredible job of sharing biblical truths in his art, whether you would realize it or not. And most people wouldn't. They would just think he has a message of hope and love and unity.

It just so happens to be that the root of those three traits comes from his relationship with Jesus.

Tiago was born and raised in Brazil, so he still does a lot of work throughout that country and is well respected in the art world.

One day, Tiago, our friend Ray, and I were having lunch at a little poke bowl spot in the art district of Miami called Wynwood. Tiago had hinted about a project he was working on in the past, but today he was ready to unfold the entire plan to us.

Turn an abandoned church building in Cuiaba, Brazil, into a functional art piece.

I was sold. I said, "Bro, I'm coming with you no matter what, even if it's to just clean your spray can tips."

Ray said the same thing. Two months later we were boarding a flight to South America.

Cuiaba is a small city on the west side of Brazil, and it has this very cool little art community. The abandoned church project was being sponsored by a gallery there, Sic Bartão, literally the nicest people ever.

For ten days straight we would drive an hour into the farmland to a small church on the side of the road, and Tiago would work on his masterpiece, while Ray and I lent helping hands.

On the final day, we closed out our time there by holding a church service. You see, the church in Brazil is very divided. But we were in town to bring unity. So our service consisted of a Catholic priest and an Evangelical pastor each sharing a word and then taking communion together, to dedicate the revived building to the Lord.

Before leaving for the airport, we made our last stop at the art gallery to say good-bye to everyone.

And there it was. A statue of Jesus that was the best thing I've ever seen.

He was smiling with two thumbs up. And it was pink. I thought, *This is what it's all about*, and also, *I need it*. I didn't have room in my luggage, but you better believe I carried that thing in my hands for the next twenty-four hours as we made our way back to Miami.

That happy Jesus statue now sits in my office, and instead of being disappointed with me, he says,

> Hey man, you got this.
> I love you.
> You are worthy.
> Keep smiling.
> Keep making the world a better place.
> I'm proud of you.
> Don't stop.

The Happiest Person Ever

So in case you still wonder, Jesus was actually happy.

He didn't walk around with eyes of judgment, telling everyone that they were going to hell.

He didn't change water to wine and then keep the party going just so he could tell everyone to stop drinking.

He didn't share stories about throwing mountains into the sea and logs stuck inside your eye without giggling a little bit—at least internally.[3]

No, he was the life of the party, telling people, "You're welcome into the kingdom. You don't have to prove anything. I love you." Why else would all these sinners and children and women love being around him?

I guarantee none of these people would want to spend time with Jesus if he was boring, pessimistic, and judgmental.

So why do so many of us rarely associate our religious identity with joy? Instead, we often pair it with sin and judgment. I completely agree that both things are important to discuss and be aware of, but I wonder if we subconsciously begin to associate every story from the Bible with that, instead of believing that Jesus really did free us from our bondage.

It's as if there is an already established set of emotions and postures of self-hatred that gets imprinted into our psyche, and yet we expect to see the world as God sees it?

Which is really from a place of goodness and joy and restoration, not from a place of destruction and sadness.

But we wouldn't know any better unless we were taught these things. Or studied the Bible for ourselves.

We can't pour bleach on a plant and expect it to grow into joy.

We need to groom it from the seed to understand that love and goodness and gratitude and forgiveness are what will grow into joy.

Just because you were raised with a certain mindset doesn't mean that it's true.

Jesus has risen! The tomb is empty!

And while an empty tomb might be a better symbol for Christianity than a cross, it doesn't look as cool. The tomb is necessary, though, because the tomb was opened. It was empty! We must live in that reality. We must understand our faith from a resurrection standpoint, not strictly in view of the cross.

The tomb is open.

The future is open.

We must live as though anything can happen now because we know that God didn't abandon Jesus to death.

On the other hand, when we live as though Jesus remains on the cross, there is a fixedness to the world. We go about our life, have fun, sin a little, go to church on Sunday, and Jesus is still there bearing the weight of our sin.

This doesn't allow for an alternative imagination to develop and co-create alongside God in a post-resurrection world, which is what we are called to do.

But as you know, our view of Jesus largely impacts our relationship with him, which some of you are just hearing for the first time.

Shortly before Jesus was born, an angel approached a group of shepherds and told them, "Fear not, for behold, I bring you good news of great joy that will be for all the people."[4]

The birth of Jesus was good news, not bad news.

Those who follow him will have great joy, not sadness.

Verse after verse—from before Jesus was born, during his ministry, and after his resurrection—was all about the joy Jesus had. And how the same joy is available to us, as believers and followers of the Way.

Jesus was full of the Holy Spirit. As believers, you and I have the Holy Spirit too.

Paul taught the church in Galatia by saying, "But the fruit of the Spirit is love, joy, peace, patience, kindness, goodness, faithfulness, gentleness, self-control; against such things there is no law."[5]

Love.
Joy.
Peace.
Patience.
Kindness.
Goodness.
Faithfulness.

Gentleness.

Self-control.

Nine characteristics that are supposed to easily flow through our lives, that we are supposed to grow in every day as we become more like Jesus. He had the fullness, and we are on our way to it.

(I believe it should be our goal every day to improve in at least one of the above traits. A great starting point for self-reflection would be to go through the gratitude prompts at the end of this book.)

The fruit of the Spirit is what should come to mind when nonbelievers think of us, not judgment, rudeness, strife, and gloom.

And I think all of this begins with seeing Jesus from a different perspective. He was a funny guy. He was joyful. He was kind and loved others better than anybody else did. He handed out party invitations to everyone, not just the righteous.

I'm not sure what view of Jesus has sunk into your head, but I would encourage you to do an audit. Maybe that means you need to do some rewriting yourself. That's okay. Pray about it and ask Jesus to show you his true personality.

He loves you and he wants joy to swell up inside of you too.

Jesus in the Back Seat

Why is it that when you are in high school, you love pranking people? Was it just me, or can you relate?

I had a friend named Paul who had this old-school black Saab. Now, this wasn't your ordinary Saab. He had modified it a little bit. He put a speaker under the hood and a CB radio in the dashboard.

If you have no idea what I'm talking about, it means he could talk to truck drivers on the interstate, but he could also use the microphone as a loudspeaker out of the hood of his car.

This was a problem.

He would drive up and down Main Street while I lay in the back seat, microphone in hand. Paul would tell me under his breath what was happening on the street around us, and I would give a little commentary on the situation, all while he kept a straight face.

Dog walkers, people in line at the movie theater or at the bus stop . . .

Nobody was safe.

I would say one outlandish thing after the next, trying to get Paul to blow his cover. But he was a professional. No comment could make that face crack.

Then we would pull off to a side street and bust out laughing, envisioning everything that was running through the poor civilians' minds.

I had another best friend in high school named Dave (same Dave who ate in the classroom with me).

Dave's car was also modified—just a little differently from Paul's.

He had Christmas lights on the inside of it. No matter what street we pulled down, the Christmas cheer followed.

One night we were driving around town when I noticed that Dave had one of those extremely bright flashlights in the back seat. You know, the ones that require like ten D-batteries and have thousands of candlepower pumping out of them.

I thought it would be funny to start shining it at people and at houses. Bad idea.

As Dave drove down the street and I blazed the flashlight off in the distance, I noticed there were lights aside from mine moving back and forth. Confused as could be, I turned around to see if someone else was doing the same thing I was.

And, well, they kind of were.

But it was a cop.

And we were being pulled over.

The good news is that they didn't even notice the flashlight.

The bad news is that you aren't allowed to have Christmas lights on inside your car, I guess. What an odd rule.

Those were such fun times. We laughed constantly back then. But then, as you get older, things often change. Our views of the world change. What's important to us changes. We become more serious. And many people settle.

Jesus doesn't change like we do.

He was the same back then as he is today. And he was fun then. I think Jesus would have been sitting in Paul's and Dave's back seats with me. Laughing.

In the Gospel of John, when Jesus is telling his disciples about all of the things to come, he says, "These things I have spoken to you, that my joy may be in you, and that your joy may be full."[6] The joy Jesus had was going to be passed on to his disciples. If Jesus was boring, this statement wouldn't have mattered. But he wasn't. The disciples wanted to attain the level of joy Jesus so graciously displayed.

And Jesus offers the same joy to you and me.

G. K. Chesterton once said, "Joy, which was the small publicity of the pagans, is the gigantic secret of the Christian."[7] People should be looking at us, wondering where our joy comes from and how they can get a little for themselves.

Heaven is overflowing with joy and laughter.

Can you imagine how unattractive eternity would be without it?

PART TWO

HOW TO LIVE IT OUT

CHAPTER 7

Feel All the Feels

I GREW UP IN MINNESOTA, the Land of 10,000 Lakes. There are actually about 12,000 lakes, but the number 10,000 seems more marketable. So that's what we go with.

I may be biased, but I think it's one of the best places in the world. It reminds you of a breath of fresh air. Everyone who visits me is always shocked by how much they like Minnesota, especially my friends who live in big cities like New York, Los Angeles, and Miami. They always leave saying, "Man, I could really see myself living here."

Unless they come during winter months.

Now, that's an entirely different story.

That story consists of, "I don't know how anybody would ever choose to live in this," and potentially some bad words thrown out on the way from our house to the car.

But the key to living up here is that you just don't talk about those months very often.

They're the odd uncle of the family months.

You especially don't talk about those months if you're trying to get someone to move here (as I did with my wife). No, you show them the carrot. You make them fall in love with the lake life and the leaves changing and the cabins and bonfires. You know, the types of things you see in movies.

I worked at different coffee shops and restaurants for years. I always loved working in customer-facing roles because of the flexibility and great money, and because it was my sole responsibility to make sure people had a good time.

I have positivity and optimism etched into my DNA, so the latter of those was easy for me.

But working in those environments also allowed me to understand how uncommon a personality trait that is. Most people have to work hard to be positive and optimistic. It doesn't come naturally.

People asked me constantly, "Zach, how are you so joyful all the time?"

And I didn't really have an answer. I would say, "I don't know. I just am."

I guess deep down, I knew how much worse life could be and how unrealistic it is that you and I are alive.

I also knew Jesus. Sort of.

I grew up going to church and calling myself a Christian. (A lot of people in America do the same thing just because it's an easy answer on government questionnaires.)

My life often projected values I was taught in church, but there were some Christians I didn't want to be associated with—especially a girl I worked with named Jenny. She was a little weird.

We worked at the same coffee shop. Her faith probably had nothing to do with her weirdness, but it definitely didn't help the scenario, because everyone associated the two with each other.

Jenny was super prophetic, and that made things worse. She would share dreams and prophetic words with other employees, myself included, and behind her back, we would talk about how strange it was. Now, today I believe the gifts of the Spirit are necessary for building up the Body of Christ, but back then it was a different story.

It creeped me out.

We worked with another person whose name tag said Michael, but he preferred to go by his alter ego, Charlie Angel.

Charlie Angel was Buddhist. And he was also one of the kindest people you could ever meet. His heart was gold.

Being surrounded by Jenny and Charlie Angel every day sure didn't help as I was going through my own spiritual quarter-life crisis.

What do I really believe?

Is this stuff actually real?

Do I want to be associated with people like Jenny?

Or do I just want people to feel loved and appreciated?

These were all questions running through my mind. I hadn't been to church in nearly two years because I couldn't grasp being around people who weren't living out what they were being taught. So in reality, I don't think my doubts were ever about God, they were only brought on by other people. And we are seeing the same thing with the deconstruction movement right now. People are turning away from God because of something a *person* did or said, not something God did.

But it's not always easy to separate the two in your mind.

As I was processing which direction I wanted to go with my faith, I got fired.

Well, we all did. The coffee shop was to be torn down and turned into condominiums.

Not only that, but a company I was building as a side hustle was falling through, I wasn't anywhere near the place in life that I expected to be at twenty-six, and I had just broken up with my girlfriend.

Each one of those would have been manageable by itself, but the culmination of all four at once hit me like a sack of bricks.

I remember sitting outside in the parking lot, crying in my car, questioning everything.

God, are you real?

If so, are you actually good?

Do you care about me?

Why do bad things happen?

How am I so far behind in life?

Something in me was stirring, I just didn't know what. That night I decided I was going to give two years to God: I would study. I would pray. I would do everything possible to figure out if he is who all these Christians say he is. And after two years, if nothing changed, I would be done with my faith as it was.

Six months later, I moved to Australia to study the Bible through a super-intensive nine-month program. And during my time out there is when everything changed for me.

It's Okay to Doubt

The more I've grown, the more I realize that my doubts weren't a bad thing at all. They were the catalyst that brought me to this place today.

Doubting is completely normal. It makes you human.

We can stop pretending that everything is okay all the time and that there is always a solid answer. Sometimes there isn't. Sometimes questioning things is necessary.

What matters is what the doubt turns into.

And hopefully it's something beneficial.

The Gospel writer Matthew shares a story about what took place right after Jesus' resurrection. He said that the eleven disciples went to Galilee to meet Jesus on the mountain, just as he had directed them. Matthew described it by saying, "When they saw him they worshiped him, but some doubted."[1]

Some worshiped Jesus.

Some doubted Jesus.

It's not like this was some ideological thing that some of the disciples may not have been on board with yet. This was Jesus' resurrection. He had just come back from the dead. This was the big aha moment, not something that should be glossed over.

But still, some of the disciples stood at a distance and doubted.

How beautiful that Matthew included this statement.

And Jesus' response was even more beautiful. He was silent about it. He went on to commission the disciples out into the world.

Jesus didn't judge them or yell at them or tell them the "right" way to think. No, he allowed them to process and question and doubt what was going on. There was room for all of it.

Some days life is good, and some days life is messed up. We shouldn't cover the bad just to protect our image. Experiencing both is what it means to be human.

SOME DAYS LIFE
IS GOOD AND
SOME DAYS LIFE
IS MESSED UP.
EXPERIENCING BOTH
IS WHAT IT MEANS
TO BE HUMAN.

It's healthy to question things. We can't pretend that the Bible is clear-cut on every topic. In reality, there are gray areas, and as a result, churches have split and there are thousands of denominations. If we don't allow room for doubt, it will eat us on the inside and cause a whole bunch of weak Christianese answers to important questions instead of thought-out, well-articulated responses.

If you have questions, that's okay.

If you have concerns, that's okay.

If you are doubting everything, that's okay.

That means you are human. Celebrate the journey you are on. There's no shame in it.

So take those questions, concerns, and doubts and turn them into something beneficial. It's not like you're the first person to have them. Study, pray, listen to God. Make space for all of it. This is a time to get closer to him in a real way. Between you and him alone.

Jesus finished the Great Commission by saying, "I am with you always, to the end of the age."[2]

To the believers and to the doubters.

He said, "I am with you."

No matter how far we may veer off the path, Jesus is still there with us.

It's Okay to Grieve

I want to be very clear when I talk about seeing the good and having an optimistic outlook on life. I am not suggesting that you suppress your feelings the slightest bit. It is completely normal and wholly important to feel all the feels. If you're dealing with some really hard things in life, that's understandable, and you should take time to grieve.

This book is about pushing to the other side of those emotions once you've worked through them and experience a sense of hope.

David Benner once said, "It is relatively easy to meet God in moments of joy or bliss. In these situations we correctly count ourselves blessed by God. The challenge is to believe that this is also true—and to know God's presence—in the midst of doubt, depression, anxiety, conflict or failure. But the God who is Immanuel is equally in those moments we would never choose as in those we would always gladly choose."[3]

Remember, Jesus said, "I am with you always, to the end of the age." Not, "I am with you when things are good" or, "I am with you when you want me to be." No, he said, "I am with you always." When good things are happening and when bad things are happening. He is there.

The Bible is full of texts that are meant to come alongside you when times get tough. These passages acknowledge that sadness and despair are a necessary part of the human experience, and help us process that. Many times, there isn't a particular meaning behind our suffering or an answer to why it's happening; it's more a result of what it means to be human. Bad things happen to good people because we live in a sinful world. What's important is how we interact with the suffering and what we allow to come from it.

Know that you are not alone. Regardless of the experience, the biblical writer identifies and provides a home for those who are wandering through difficult moments of intense darkness.

A lot of the time there isn't an answer, but there is hope for what's to come.

Lamentations is a small book of the Bible that is often skipped over because people don't really know what to do with the pain and suffering, which is what this book is all about.

It's actually a book of five poems that took place right after the siege of Jerusalem in 587 BC. The Babylonians had just come into the city and completely destroyed everything, taking the first round of Israelites into exile.

There was blood and fire and smoke and tears. It wasn't a pretty sight.

The author of Lamentations walks through the rubble. Remembering what once was. Questioning everything. Living in confusion.

"How in the world could God have allowed this to happen to his people?"

And so he cried and was angry and bitter and yelled at God for answers. But there weren't any.

For some reason, sharing emotions like the author's can be uncomfortable for us because we see a lot of other Christians who seem to have their lives together. So we put on a show when we're around them and pretend everything is fine, even when sometimes it isn't. Even when sometimes all you want to do is cry and get angry and yell at God, "Why?!"

Well, guess what? God isn't afraid of that. He actually encourages it in his Word, which is why books such as Lamentations and Psalms have been kept around for so long: to teach us how to grieve properly.

Through our grief is how we find true healing.

So let it out. Work your way through it. Allow your tears to cleanse yourself of all that has been pushed down for too long.

It's normal to grieve. It's not normal to pretend everything is fine all the time when it isn't. Go all the way in and let it out. In the big picture, seasons only last a short time. They come and they go.

Seasons can also be terrifying because the beginning of every new season means that an old season is coming to an end. And there's no correct way to process it. For some of us it's easy, for others it's quite difficult.

My wife and I recently moved to Minneapolis after spending two years in Miami. We didn't expect to move so quickly, but sometimes things work out that way and you just need to go. We didn't really have time to process what was going on because it happened so fast. One day we were living in sunshine and paradise, and the next day we were raking fallen leaves, getting ready for snow to fall.

Sometimes it's a move that forces a new season.

Sometimes it's a job loss.

Sometimes it's a divorce.

Whatever pain you might be going through, know that with every end is a new beginning and that God is there with you in the midst of it. Just as in all new creation stories, something must die in order for something else to be born. There is no going back to the way things were. So keep your focus in front of you and accept all that God is giving you in this new season.

For some people it might help to mark those seasons in some way. In the Bible, we see people building altars and putting stones down to remember where they have come from and how God has stepped in.

What are some ways you can mark such moments in your life?

Maybe it's by purchasing a piece of art or pottery.

Maybe it means writing about the moments so you can one day pass down your memories to your grandchildren.

Personally, I'm a tattoo guy. So for me, when big things happen in my life, I like to get a tattoo to represent the turning moment and faithfulness of God. For instance, I have a big whale on my forearm. I call it my Jonah tattoo because for years I was running from the Lord, but he was chasing after me the whole time. Above the whale are the coordinates to where I lived in Australia because that was such a defining moment in my relationship with him.

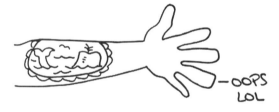

No matter what you have gone through, just know this . . .

On the other side of doubt
and pain
and questions
is hope.

But you have to keep pushing through, otherwise you'll be stuck in the mess forever.

Use the pain and become stronger.

Use the doubt and learn more.

Use the past season to push you forward into a healthy new season.

We need to learn how to be grateful for where we've been and hopeful for where we are going.

I spent a week in Jackson Hole, Wyoming, a few years back with an incredible group of people. A few guys from my city invited us to go on adventures together and talk about Jesus. I was sold.

My friend Matt and I went out there together; no matter the itinerary, we were ready to conquer it. And conquer it we did.

Day one: fly fishing.

Day two: horseback riding.

Day three: hiking.

It was on day three when the trip began to conquer me.

Our group met at 7 a.m. to hike up the Grand Tetons. It was a dream morning. We tied our hiking boots extra tight, put on an extra layer of clothes, and were off. The peak we decided to hike up that day was roughly forty-five minutes to the top, passing deer and other wildlife on the way.

If you've ever been to the top of a mountain, it's the most breathtaking view, being able to look across the various peaks and valleys.

It's *peaceful* summed up in a snapshot.

Our guide gave the group a two-hour span of free time to either explore or pray. A group of five of us came to the conclusion that the best thing we could do was hike down to the lake in the middle of the mountain range and go for a dip, even though there was a light snowfall dusting the air.

On our way down to the lake, we heard one of the other guys yell from the distance, "BEAR!"

So we all stopped. My heart was racing. And all ten of our eyes scanned the scenery for any sort of movement. Then, about twenty yards away, a small brown bear walked by, most likely trying to find his mother.

We kept going and eventually made it to the sand beach between two mountaintops. The crystal water was magical.

I'm not going to lie, at this point I was on the verge of chickening out. It was cold. And remember, I really don't like being cold and wet.

Well, three of the guys convinced me to go in, while my friend Matt stayed on dry land shooting a video of the experience.

We all stripped down to our underwear and took off running. My plan was to go in only a few feet because the water was freezing, but the momentum kept me moving until I was fully submerged. At one point, my knee buckled for some reason, but I couldn't tell why because my feet were numb.

When we got back to shore, I looked at the ground, and there was blood spilling out of my foot. Not from a little cut either.

I could stick my finger in the slice.

We were in the middle of a mountain range, so I started to freak out. I thought I was going to have to be helicoptered out of there.

Matt was a professional at staying calm under pressure, so he brought me back to reality and we had to come up with a solution, pronto. One guy gave me his bandana to tie around my foot to stop the bleeding. Another gave me a protein bar. And Matt gave me his shoulder to lean on as we began our ascent up and over the mountain, forty-five minutes in each direction.

If it hadn't been for Matt, I wouldn't have made it.

Matt was in remission from cancer at the time, but he still lent out his energy to help me.

Shortly after the trip, Matt's cancer came back full force, and it didn't end the way we all were praying it would. I wasn't around for Matt toward the end. He was kind of a superhero to me, so I just expected he would make it. I didn't return the favor and let him lean on me when he was limping. And that's something I deal with often.

What causes you to limp in life?

What do you need to lean into to get through tough seasons?

Whether it's leaning on someone else or allowing another person to lean on you, don't find yourself in the position of regretting it when it's too late. Jump in the water with those around you and just be there for them, helping each other no matter the situation.

That's Where Joy Comes In

This is where joy comes into play. It's on the other side of heartache. It's when you push all the way through, experiencing all the emotions you can possibly experience, and all you have left is a sense of relief.

Joy is present there.

You can breathe again and smile, and laugh once or twice.

Life is fragile and some things are very hard. But you and I are here today. We have a shot at this thing called life. We can choose to make the best of it or the worst. And with Jesus, your joy can be everlasting.

Tim Keller often talks about how silly it is to establish your joy in things that can be taken away. He argues that the world thinks joy can be found in the things of this world. This is because we have bursts of joy here and there, but we are left looking for a joy that endures. He illustrates this point through C. S. Lewis's record of his pursuit of joy in his autobiography, *Surprised by Joy*. In it, Lewis writes of finding fleeting joy in books and friends—two great things.

But eventually, Lewis found Jesus.

Now he knew that all the other joys were but signposts leading the way to Jesus. Keller explains Lewis's argument:

> He says if you are lost in the woods and you first come upon a signpost, it's a big deal. The one who first sees the signpost in the woods says, "Look!" The whole party gathers around and states and says, "Ah, finally. That's the direction." But if you've found the road and if you're passing signposts every few miles, you don't stop and stare at the signposts. They encourage you, and you will be grateful to the authority that set them up.
>
> "But we shall not stop and stare, or not much . . . though their pillars are of silver and their lettering of gold." Why because, "'We would be at Jerusalem.'" Do you see the point? He says if you really are lost, when you find a signpost, you get pretty excited about it. But when you know your way, when you know the thing to which the signposts point, that's where you're on your way. You don't stop and look at the signposts.[4]

Keller summarizes what Lewis was getting at:

> What he realizes is food, friends, success, acclaim, popularity, money . . . all the things that we think, "If I have that, that's going to give me the joy," are signposts. So enjoy them. Some of them are great! Some of them are made of silver with letters of gold. But don't mistake the signposts for what they're signaling, the thing they're pointing to, which is the city of God, which is God himself. That gets you out of either being afraid of enjoying

things in this life or, at the same time, resting your heart too much in them.[5]

So enjoy your life. God created us to be joyful human beings. As believers, we are examples of Jesus on earth.

In order for people to want what we have, we need to be joyful,
hopeful,
grateful,
loving,
and a positive influence on society, not just for ourselves, but because these actions reverberate throughout culture and can have transformative impacts.

It would be a disservice for us to live any differently.

A few years ago, I was invited to work at a dinner party for one of our clients. This house was massive. The left half of the house was the living quarters, while the right half was the event side, stocked and ready to go at any time.

And this time it just so happened that the Dalai Lama was in town for a luncheon.

I know, crazy.

In the basement of the entertainment side of the house was a room full of signed guitars from various people. Whether you play guitar or not, it was probably the coolest room you've ever seen.

At one point I heard laughter flooding out of the room, but I knew the workers weren't supposed to be in that room. So I peeked around the door out of curiosity, and inside were

two of the monks who had come with the
Dalai Lama, playing one of the guitars.
Not just any guitar. It was the guitar of
Gene Simmons from Kiss.

And these two monks looked up at me with
joy that stopped me in my tracks. It was the
purest, most childlike joy I had witnessed in
a long time, making me burst with happiness inside.

You know how awesome it is to see
someone else having the time of their
life? It makes you so happy in return. And by sharing your joy it helps
other people lighten the load they are
carrying.

This is what it means to be human.

GENE SIMMONS
GUITAR

To feel everything.
To ask questions.
To get angry.
To grieve.
To lament.

But when it's all said and done, the end result should be
joy, peace, love, and gratitude.

CHAPTER 8

See the Good

THE SPREAD OF COVID-19 placed the entire world on hold in 2020, with ramifications leading into the following years, if not the entire decade. Everything is different now.

I'm pretty sure the word *pivot* will never be the same.

Every person, every business, everything needed to learn how to pivot.

Gisela and I got engaged about a month before the world shut down. So we needed to learn how to pivot our love story unless we wanted to be engaged indefinitely. But I was trying to wife that up.

One afternoon, Gisela and I, along with my friends Caleb and Anthony, were all working out of our apartment living room. Complications for getting a marriage license were the last thing on our minds, until Anthony shared that all of the government buildings in Miami closed down.

We were planning on getting married a month later and now didn't know if we would be able to get a marriage license.

I called the closest office, and their response was basically that I was out of luck.

I called the next county over. Same response.

The next county, same thing.

Uh-oh.

I called every county in Florida, and the only one that was open at the time was in Fort Myers, a two-hour drive away, and they were closing the following day.

We dropped everything, hopped in my car, and began a hilarious drive across the peninsula.

When the day arrived for our actual wedding a month later, we also had to pivot.

Because the world was shut down, and no groups of seven or more were allowed to gather, we found a city park a few miles from our house and set up shop. It was literally a pastor, G's parents, our friend Caleb, and us, with my parents on FaceTime.

Definitely not the ideal situation, but it was perfect.

What made it even harder was that because my mom is immunocompromised, we had to wait through an entire year of quarantine before we could even hug my parents. Thankfully, we were able to visit Minnesota every month to see them in person, but it was always at a distance and always outside.

We would go to a park and eat pizza at separate picnic benches.

We would go fishing but stand on different docks.

When winter hit, we had to modify it a little bit. We would go on walks around the block or go snowshoeing or sit in the garage bundled up in snow gear because winters in Minnesota are on another level.

We pivoted, but the shared experience brought us closer.

Another thing that brought G and I closer during quarantine was getting a dog. We picked up Nyla in Philadelphia when she was eight weeks old. In hindsight, we had no idea what we were doing. Neither G nor I had grown up with a puppy, and no matter how many books you read or videos you watch, until you're in the thick of it, you don't understand.

Can I get an amen?

Night one, Nyla was exhausted from traveling, so I was pretty confident she was going to sleep for a while. We put her in her crate, turned on a YouTube playlist titled "15 HOURS of Deep Separation Anxiety Music for Dog Relaxation! Helped 4 Million Dogs Worldwide! New!" and I don't know why, but I thought we were good.

And we were good.

For about an hour.

That's when the anxiety began to kick in, even though the YouTube video clearly claimed it wouldn't. So I moved out to sleep on the couch next to her crate.

Which worked.

For an hour.

Then I moved to the floor. But that wasn't close enough. Nyla needed to be touching me. So I draped my arm over the playpen, tossing and turning for the rest of the night.

I woke up (well, not that I really was ever sleeping), but I "woke up" at 5 a.m., lying on our tile floor with a tiny pillow, no blanket, my arm numb from losing circulation, music playing on YouTube, and I'm not kidding, I just started to cry.

I was miserable. I was questioning everything. Like, I Googled what the return policy was on puppies. I was done.

But if you've had a puppy, you know that each day gets a little easier, and the love you have for that furball makes it all worth it.

After a year of waiting to hug my parents, the country began to reopen, and my mom and dad were comfortable being around others in person. G and I booked the first ticket we could find so they could hug their daughter-in-law after waiting so long. We pulled up to their house with Nyla in hand and they came running outside, squeezing us for way longer than would normally be acceptable, and we all began to cry.

The good kind of tears.

You see, having an attitude of gratitude means you figure out how to make lemonade out of lemons.

You don't worry about what tomorrow brings but celebrate what's happening today.

You always focus on the silver lining of the situation.

And gratitude connects us to others and to God.

Life Is a Gift

For a lot of people, it's difficult to see how life can be considered a gift, because that means they'd need to acknowledge the Giver. Most people want to make it seem like we don't need someone else's help. We take pride in our independence.

The Jewish tradition has an inspiring view of gratitude that I think every person, no matter your religion, can learn something from. Every day it is the goal of those who practice this to recite one hundred blessings, or thanks, to God, beginning with eighteen blessings right when they wake up in the morning.

The view is that as you are sleeping, your soul leaves your body, and what better way to come back to reality upon waking than to recite eighteen blessings.

Why eighteen?

Because in Judaism, each letter is represented by a number, a system called *gematria*, and numbers/letters placed together create a word. In this case, the number eighteen is a combination of the letters *chet* and *yud*, creating the word *chai* (pronounced khai).

Chai means life.

So the reason many Jewish people begin their day with eighteen blessings is because they are grateful for another day of life.

Grateful for clothes to wear.

Eyes to see.

Feet to stand on.

Strength to carry themselves.

The list goes on, and throughout the day there are over a hundred total blessings shared.

Imagine how different our view of life would be if we said one hundred things we were grateful for each and every day. It would automatically ground us, and we would have much more clarity on the big picture. We would see that God's hand over everything is a gift. Everything. From the depths of creation to the smallest moment.

He has his hand in every created thing we see and do not see. God is telling us to look around and see all of the good things he is doing. So often we turn into grumblers, complaining about the most trivial life events. Yes, there are plenty of bad things happening around us in the world, but it is our responsibility to make them better instead of worse. We have the choice each day to focus on taking actions and building disciplines that will bring the kingdom closer.

Jesus' brother, James, teaches us that every good gift is from God.[1] Every single one of them.

Sunshine.

Another breath.

Food.

Children.

All good. All gifts.

The biggest mistake in the world is having a mindset that any of this is owed to us. We need to shift our attitude to a place of gratitude today, not tomorrow. Not when we're sick and finally appreciate good health. Not when things are bad financially and we appreciate what we did have.

No, let's be people who learn to appreciate every single thing now.

Just saying "thank you" is one of the simplest forms of prayer but brings us closer to God in new levels. Thanking him for the big things and small things. Admitting that the source of all goodness is him, not anything we do.

And the more we give thanks to God, the more we see him moving in our lives. An object in motion stays in motion; it's that type of situation. The more God's goodness is on our minds, the stronger our sense of it will become. We will begin to see him moving in and around us constantly. His presence will become all the greater, allowing us to appreciate what is right here.

Either God is present in every moment, or he isn't.

Which do you believe?

Some of us need a complete attitude shift. What we look for we will find. If we believe God is good and we are constantly grateful for all he is doing in our lives, we are going to see him more. And the opposite is true as well.

As we grow in our relationship with Jesus, the Holy Spirit empowers us and helps us with the process of renewing our minds so we can see things from a different perspective—from his perspective. We'll see what is important and what isn't. We'll realize that there is so much more going on here than what it might seem like.

Now when we spill coffee on our pants or we get cut off in traffic, it isn't as big a deal.

Psychologists have been discussing the effects of gratitude for the longest time. Not only does gratitude impact our relationship with God, but it also improves our well-being.[2]

Gratitude is known to:

Increase self-esteem.
Make people like us.
Make us more optimistic.
Improve friendships.
Improve romantic relationships.
Improve sleep.
Improve decision making.
Relieve stress.
Reduce blood sugar.
The list goes on and on and on.[3]

In Luke 17:11–19, the author shares a story about Jesus' interaction with a group of ten lepers.

It reads, "On the way to Jerusalem [Jesus] was passing along between Samaria and Galilee. And as he entered a village, he was met by ten lepers, who stood at a distance and lifted up their voices saying, 'Jesus, Master, have mercy on us.' When he saw them he said to them, 'Go and show yourselves to the priests.'"[4]

Because in those days, in order to be accepted back into society, you needed to have a priest declare you clean. Priests were considered a credible source and would have acknowledged the miracle that had taken place.

The story continues, "And as they went they were cleansed. Then one of them, when he saw that he was healed, turned back, praising God with a loud voice; and he fell on his face at Jesus' feet, giving him thanks. Now he was a Samaritan."[5]

Side note: Jewish people hated Samaritans. The fact that Jesus calls out the good that a Samaritan is doing, time and time again, would have been very aggravating to the Jewish audience.

"Then Jesus answered, 'Were not ten cleansed? Where are the nine? Was no one found to return and give praise to God except this foreigner?' And he said to him, 'Rise and go your way; your faith has made you well.'"[6]

All ten of them were healed. Jesus didn't lay hands on them. He told them to go, and in their obedience—the action of going—they were all healed physically.

What's amazing to note is that to the one man who came back, Jesus said, "Your faith has made you well," often translated as "made whole." Physical healing isn't the goal—wholeness is, which consists of physical, mental, and spiritual wellness.

Their obedience brought physical healing.

This guy's faith brought wholeness.

The Samaritan's gratitude for what Jesus did boosted his faith.

Living with a heart of gratitude boosts our faith and brings us into greater wholeness—physically, mentally, and spiritually.

The more grateful we are, the more we'll see God in every-thing and how he is moving all around us. It's a choice we get to make daily. There are 86,400 seconds in a day; it's not going to hurt to take a few of those seconds and thank him for all he has blessed us with.

A Sense of Wonder

Being raised in Minnesota, I started snowboarding at a pretty young age. Like, the first time I rode a board was when I was nine. My cousin got one for Christmas that year and brought it over for me to try.

I was hooked.

But as I grew older, my friends became better and better, trying more daring tricks, and truthfully, I didn't have the guts for most of them. I would do jumps and grind boxes if they were only a few feet off the ground, but the thought of falling hard on concrete while riding down rails in the middle of the city gave me the chills.

Did you know that Minnesota's snow is different from the snow in the mountains? We have big hills and get lots of snow, but it's either wet and soggy or it freezes over and becomes harder than a rock. Most of the time we actually just have machines making snow and shooting it over the hills. The first time I was introduced to fresh powder, it was a game changer.

One of my favorite places to go snowboarding is Whitefish Mountain Resort on Big Mountain in Montana. My friends and I usually rent what's called a ski-in, ski-out home, which is basically a house on the side of the mountain, so you don't have to travel to the resort every day. It's just right there.

What I love most about snowboarding on fresh powder is feeling like I'm surfing on land.

The best thing to do is go off the groomed path and head into the woods, carving back and forth between the trees. You need to make sure you have a helmet on and goggles down, though, because those branches come at you quick!

During one of our trips to Whitefish, my friend Connor riding early in the morning before the rest of us woke up. While we were cooking breakfast, he returned with a peculiar look in his eyes, and all he was saying was, "I found Jesus."

I mean, Connor went to a Christian university, so I guess I just figured he was already a believer, but at this moment he was acting strange. Eyes wide, he wouldn't say anything else or explain himself. I thought he was messing with us, or that someone spiked his coffee on the chairlift, because it was weird.

The rest of us were looking at each other like, *This dude has lost his mind.* But he hadn't.

We strapped on our boards, and he took us to the place he found. On the front side of the mountain, tucked into the woods, was a seven-foot-tall statue of Jesus.

Connor wasn't lying.

We sat on the mountain, looking out across the majesty of God's creation next to Jesus. Breathing. Slowly nodding our heads, thinking, *Wow, he made all of this for our enjoyment. How incredible.*

If you want to meet Jesus, go to Whitefish, Montana. He's definitely there.

God is just as present in the physical as he is in the spiritual.

I often hear Christians dismiss the physical and try to explain that the spiritual life is all that's important. This is called Gnosticism—the separation of flesh and spirit—and it was seen as heresy in the early church.

Ancient Greek thought was more concerned with the spirit over the flesh. The spirit was seen as something that was purely good and beautiful, while the flesh was considered dirty and temporal.

Early Christian communities flirted heavily with Gnosticism, and in response it took about four hundred years to be removed from church doctrine.

Yes, we want to be fully devoted to God by transforming our actions and habits, but God also gave us a body! It was God who became incarnate in the form of Jesus to save us.

So it isn't about denying our body, but more so, the purest expression of the body is one that is entirely devoted to God. And he is moving all around us in the day-to-day.

One of our roles as Christians is to open our eyes, to stand in the awe and wonder of our great God in the physical. Bad things happen when we lose our sense of wonder, when we are no longer astonished at the goodness of God.

And as we see God moving all around us, we should respond with a sense of worship and praise, thanking him for all things.

God created everything, and all of creation is around us. You would think it would be easy to keep that sense of awe and wonder, but for some reason it isn't that simple. Some of us, including myself, lose that feeling over time. It happens. We get distracted by things.

I have found that three directives have helped me to keep and grow my sense of awe and wonder that might help you as well:

Slow down,
Open your eyes,
Count it all joy.

Slow Down

There is a story in the book of Exodus many of you might know very well. It's a story of Moses when he is living in the wilderness of Midian with his wife and her family. At this point, Moses was no longer Egyptian royalty. He was a shepherd for his father-in-law, Jethro.[7]

One day, as Moses was shepherding the flock, he took them out to Horeb, the mountain of God.

As he was moseying along (see what I did there?), he came across a bush that was on fire but was not being consumed. He didn't know what to do, but when he turned to go closer, the Lord spoke to Moses through the flame, telling him to take off his shoes because the ground he was standing on was holy.

This was Moses' first inter-action with God. Even though Moses was a Hebrew and his people were slaves in Egypt, Moses had been blessed with a seat in Egyptian royalty for the first season of his life. But not anymore. Moses is meeting YHWH for the first time and is told of all the amazing things God is going to accomplish through his life.

An interesting Jewish interpretation of this text discusses that the bush had actually been burning for a long time, and that it was just in this moment that Moses finally no-ticed it.[8]

We can get so caught up in our daily lives, always on the go, moving a million miles a minute, that we fail to notice the miraculous moments when God is present right in front of us.

Alice Walker in her novel *The Color Purple* wrote, "I think it pisses God off if you walk by the color purple in a field somewhere and don't notice it. . . . People think pleasing

God is all God cares about. But any fool living in the world can see it always trying to please us back. . . . It always making little surprises and springing them on us when us least expect it."[9]

How often do we walk past burning bushes and not realize it?

I don't want to be like that anymore.

I want to be present. I want to slow down and witness the godly moments in my life. I want to answer the call of God by saying what Moses said: "Here I am."

Use me, God, use me.

Open Your Eyes

Since my snowboarding friends were more focused on doing tricks off large jumps and riding rails in the city, I had to supplant my fear of falling on concrete with photography. I figured that if I wanted to remain in the culture and be a part of the coolness, I had to contribute in some way. Photos were the key.

Snowboard photography back then was a little different than it is today.

Today you can buy a nice digital camera for a few hundred bucks. Back then, when I was in high school, that wasn't an option.

I got into film photography and developing my own photos. I was lucky enough to have the choice of electives and took all the photography classes I could—so many that I could come up with my own projects. Senior year came around, and I set a goal of getting one of my photos published in a local snowboarding magazine.

I shot roll after roll of local snowboarders I didn't really know at the hill by my house. They were doing all these tricks I wished I could do, and I was right next to them with my camera.

Click.

Click.

Click.

The whole process of photography fascinated me—not just taking the photos.

In class, we would prepare the negatives and develop the shots we liked best. (We couldn't take hundreds of shots and see the result right away as we can now.) There was an art behind it. Each shot was important, but the way you developed it was also important.

The image was on the photo paper, but you couldn't see it right away.

It wasn't until you mixed the paper with the right chemicals for the perfect amount of time that the photo would appear.

The image was there, but it took the proper attention to detail to see it.

By the end of the semester, I submitted a few of my favorite photos to our local snowboard magazine, and the editor chose to use them. I was ecstatic.

But the real lesson here is in developing—realizing what is there before it is visible.

Not only do we need to learn to slow down, but we also need open our eyes and be aware of God's presence and movement in our life. If we really believe he is present at all times, it would be a disgrace to ignore him.

Count It All Joy

When Gisela and I got married, she gifted me a gold necklace with a cross on one side and our life motto on the other:

Count it all joy.

It is pulled from James 1:2–4, which says, "Count it all joy, my brothers, when you meet trials of various kinds, for you know that the testing of your faith produces steadfastness. And let steadfastness have its full effect, that you may be perfect and complete, lacking in nothing."

I wear this necklace every day as a reminder that no matter what comes my way, I am to count the blessings of every moment with a posture of joy.

Struggles in life are inevitable. Testing will come. When metals are being refined, they are placed under the flame to become purer. The fire burns away the things that weren't supposed to be there—things that were keeping it from being perfect.

When refining moments present themselves in my life, I want to be even more focused on God. When most people would push him away, I want to be aware of how he is a part of the process. My thanksgiving will turn into praise, even when praising is the last thing I want to do. But it's ever important to witness life from God's perspective, not our own.

I love how Richard Foster puts it: "God has established a created order full of excellent and good things, and it follows naturally that if we think on those things we will be happy. That is God's appointed way to joy. If we think we will have joy only by praying and singing psalms, we will be disillusioned. But if we fill our lives with simple good things and constantly thank God for them, we will know joy."[10]

We need to see things differently.

We need to see the good.

CHAPTER 9

How to Be a Blessing

"JESUS HEALED MY SOCKS and it freaked me out," said Jimmy Kellogg, known by most as Jimmy Darts.

Wait, what?! I thought to myself.

I've heard of Jesus healing people, but never a pair of socks. Who am I to judge how Jesus gets the attention of someone who is searching?

And Jimmy was searching.

Jimmy Darts grew up in a small town a few hours north of where I live in Minnesota. He was raised in the church and was taught practical ways of loving others at a young age.

For Christmas, he and his siblings would get an envelope with two hundred dollars. The first half was meant to be a gift to a homeless person, and the second half was to be spent on a present for themselves.

Generosity was a lifestyle for these kids.

Even though Jimmy saw God move in his life, he had a fire burning inside of him for something else, something crazier, so he began partying quite a bit in high school and shooting crazy videos with his friends.

At a bonfire party out in the woods one weekend, Jimmy was jumping over the fire to show off. On the way home he realized how upset his mom was going to be because there were now holes in the bottom of the socks she had just bought him, which had pictures of Jesus spread throughout the design. She definitely would have known that he was partying. And that couldn't happen.

So Jimmy prayed, *Jesus, I need you to help me*, even though he didn't know what that would entail. He got home, tucked his socks away in his underwear drawer, and went to sleep.

The next morning, when Jimmy's mom came to do his laundry, the socks were brand-new, no holes whatsoever.

It freaked him out.

The next week he came across a Billy Graham video on YouTube talking about how we all have two options: to live for yourself or to live for Jesus. In that moment, Jimmy got on his knees, repented, and rededicated his life to Jesus. He was going to find a way to direct his youthful energy and video skills into something for the kingdom, he just didn't know what that looked like yet.

As time went on, Jimmy's vision for the future grew. He wanted to start a church—but not just any church. This would be a church where people like him would want to go. Something fun. Something wild. Something like a house party.

Think waterslide baptisms, a DJ, and a raw gospel message, fueled by radical generosity. The whole church would be built on the verse that says, "The goodness of God leads men to repentance."[1] Jimmy said, "It's really just showering radical love on people, which actually melts their hearts to be able to see truth."

So how do you begin working on such a massive vision? You start by building a community of people who believe in the mission.

Jimmy spent years creating crazy videos, and he was completely fearless when it came to strangers. His parents instilled in their children to not be afraid of people on the street and to interact with them. So as an adult, no matter what city he was in, Jimmy would start talking to various homeless people, thinking, *Man, these are really cool people. A lot of them just have really unfortunate situations.*

That was the key.

He would start creating videos by positively impacting the lives of strangers.

He would just be a friend to people instead of debating theology.

He would practically live out what it meant to love others.

This was his *why*.

Now Jimmy has millions of followers on social media, and every single day he has the opportunity to bless strangers. And his followers get involved, spreading the love of Jesus, whether they believe in Jesus or not.

Like the story of a man named Yahayah. Jimmy's challenge for the day was to become best friends with a stranger. It just so happened that Yahayah felt that God told him to go to the beach the same day. So when Jimmy approached Yahayah and asked if he wanted to be best friends for the day, Yahayah immediately agreed.

Jimmy and Yahayah spent the entire day hearing each other's testimonies, roller skating, playing basketball, going out to eat, and having the time of their lives.

Now, Yahayah was homeless and on his last straw. He told Jimmy, "When you met me on the beach, you know, I was at the state in my life where I just felt like that was it for me, like I just felt like I'd rather die."

So Jimmy posted Yahayah's CashApp on social media, and it crashed because so many people wanted to help. In twenty-four hours they had raised over $30,000 to help get him out of homelessness and change his life forever.

Jimmy has a way of making people feel seen and know they are loved by God. And the ultimate goal of gaining all of these followers is to one day start the house-party church, to show people that the love and blessings he is sharing with the world every day are actually rooted in the gospel message.

It all starts with one simple act of kindness every single day.

I remember hearing about Jimmy Darts a year after I returned to the States from living in Australia, because he was part of the same Bible study program I went to, just a year behind me.

My friend Rylee was telling me about how this kid named Jimmy would raise money to go to the local toy store and buy toys for every kid who was shopping at the time. I thought it was the coolest thing ever, and even back then, with no videos to watch, I was inspired to love those around me better.

And it's my hope that Jimmy inspires you to love those around you better as well.

You Are Blessed

If the world was created by accident and our lives revolve around getting through this life to one day be transported to another world, then we will fail to recognize the gift of life. If there is no Giver, there is no gift, and life becomes meaningless.

But when gratitude is expressed, a bond is created between the Giver and the recipient. And maybe there is more going on here than meets the eye.

Creativity was heavily encouraged for me as a child because my mom was such a creative herself. Painting and jewelry were her go-to modes, so it's no surprise that I was drawn to those forms as well.

I started my first "business" as a nine-year-old while on vacation in Naples, Florida. Shark-tooth and shell necklaces were my specialty. At night I would make dozens of necklaces, and then during the day I would walk up and down the beach with an arm full of dangling beauty. (Or at least they looked cool to me.)

My passion for creating things continued over the years, through jewelry, various clothing lines, music, and books.

Using your creativity is cool, but what makes it even cooler is when you use it for a purpose.

In the summer of 1997, my mom gathered all of the neighbor kids together every week for different arts and crafts projects in hopes of having a large sale at the end of summer to donate the money to a local charity.

We made jewelry.

And ornaments.

And cards.

And pillows.

And drawings.

Every week was something different, which gave us a large supply to sell by the time summer was over.

A store down the street caught wind of what we were doing as a bunch of ten-year-olds, and they offered to sell our cards to their customers, giving us all the profit. Bonus.

The end of summer came, and we held the sale in our home. The neighbor kids and I stood around our creations with a strong sense of pride for all we had accomplished.

We turned on our "open for business" sign (in other words, unlocked the front door), and people started pulling up.

One car.

Two cars.

Dozens of cars.

We ended up selling out of our crafts and surpassed our goal of $1,000 to give to charity. We couldn't believe it. All the hard work was paying off.

The following week, my parents loaded up their cars with us kids and we took a trip to a local charity called Sharing and Caring Hands. We were able to bless them with a check, for no other reason but to share the blessing.

That experience stuck with me through the years, seeing the faces of the recipients and understanding how large an impact we can have with such little resources.

People often say, "When I'm rich I'll be able to give a bunch of it away," but in reality, we don't need to have a lot in order to give a lot.

I believe that we each are given certain gifts and responsibilities, and God sits back to see what we do with them.

For us, one small arts and crafts sale by a bunch of pre-teen kids trying to stay out of trouble during the summer made loads of difference. What has God entrusted you with in order to help others?

Jesus shares a story in Matthew 25 about a very wealthy man who was going on a long journey. While he was away, the man entrusted his wealth to his servants.

He gave one servant five bags of gold, another one two bags, and to the third servant he gave one bag, all based on what he thought each of the servants could handle. He was going to see if they knew how to cultivate and grow what they were given.

So the wealthy man went on his way, and the servants went to work.

The one who received five bags of gold began investing and quickly doubled his money. He was quite the hustler. The servant who received two bags was the same way, and he doubled his money.

But the servant who received one bag, he was different. This one buried his money out of fear that he would lose it and upset the man.

When the wealthy man returned home, he gathered the servants to see what they had done with what they were entrusted.

He was so pleased with the results of the first two men who had made extra money that he said to them, "Well done, come and share in my happiness."

But to the man who was afraid of losing his gift, the master said, "You lazy servant! Give your bag to the one with ten bags," and the man was thrown outside into the darkness.

You see, the man with one bag was afraid of the wealthy man for reasons that don't even make sense. He thought the wealthy man would punish the servants for losing what was given to them, but we don't see that anywhere in the story. From the beginning, all we see is love and generosity and abundance to even the lowest of the low—the servants. The owner gives them everything to enjoy their lives now, in excess. Not the other way around.

The stories of Jesus were so countercultural that the audience never knew what to do with them. This parable is more relevant today than ever.

How do you view God and the role we play on earth?

Do you think he is a hard boss who is always looking for you to make a mistake?

Or do you see him as joyful, loving, and asking you to participate in his happiness?

Are you just getting by?

Or are you living in abundance?

How you view God will completely impact the way you live.

Jesus is saying that this whole thing called life is a gift. We can't earn it and we don't deserve it. But what we do with it is ever important. He's saying that we have been blessed and it is our job to act like it, not live in a place of fear.

That's not always easy to do. Maybe your pastor or friend or someone you know on social media has instilled a sense of fear in you. Or maybe your parents raised you believing differently. So hearing this may make your skeptical stomach turn a little bit. But time and time again through Scripture, we see God calling his people blessed, telling them not to be fearful and to enjoy the life they have been given.

Take it one day at a time. Know that God has given you bags of gold and he wants you to participate in his happiness.

To Bless Others

I always knew I was going to be an entrepreneur in some way, so university was a little difficult for me unless it was a class that I could immediately apply to whatever project I was working on at the time.

I attended four universities in five years, with a six-month break in the middle. Looking back, I can see God's hand in all of it. But in the moment, it was a little embarrassing. Finding my calling was harder than anticipated because I just saw life so differently from everyone I was surrounded by.

And after the first two years, I decided to start fresh somewhere else: Charleston, South Carolina. The only problem was I had never been there before; I didn't even know anyone who lived within two hours of there. I actually called the local police station to ask if my apartment building was safe.

All fear aside, I packed every crevice of my 2002 Ford Explorer with the few belongings I had, and nineteen-year-old wandering spirit that I was, I moved across the country with no plan in place except to have an experience that made me want to go back to college.

The Old Testament shares a story about a man named Abraham.

Abraham wasn't just any old guy; he was considered the Father of the Jewish people. God chose Abraham to be the main figure.

In Genesis 12, we see how God called Abraham (at that time his name was Abram), saying, "Go from your country and your kindred and your father's house to the land that I will show you. And I will make of you a great nation, and I will bless you and make your name great, so that you will be a blessing. I will bless those who bless you, and him who dishonors you I will curse, and in you all the families of the earth shall be blessed."[2]

For Abram to just get up and leave would have been unheard of because back in the day, the cultures of the time were very static. You stayed in the nation you were born into. It was the same group of people your family was raised in, and their parents as well. Nobody left to chase after their dreams. It wasn't even an option.

But that's exactly what God is asking of Abram here. And Abram listens.

God promises three things:

1. Abram will be made into a great nation.
2. He will be blessed.
3. All the families of the earth will be blessed in turn.

Now, just making these promises would be one thing, but God chose to make it official with a covenant. And this type of covenant was unconditional. No matter what Abram did, God would hold up his side of the agreement.

Creating a covenant was messy business.

First, the two parties would take a sacrificial animal and cut it in half down the spine. Back then they didn't have power tools, so this process was nasty. Full of blood, sweat, and tears.

Not going to lie, it starts off a little weird.

Then the two sides of the animal would be laid on the ground facing each other, each party's family standing in groups behind the animal to "witness" the covenant.

Both parties would then walk in a figure eight around the animal halves, reciting the terms of the agreement. They would take a sharp rock, cut the palm of their hand, and shake on it, mingling the blood between the two.

Afterward, the families of both parties would have a celebration together, as their new covenant was intended to last forever.

Now, if the covenant was unconditional and one person said they would take responsibility to maintain the covenant no matter the actions of the other, only the one taking responsibility would walk through the animal halves, shouting the promises. This is what we see with God and Abram.

In Genesis 15, we read that God put Abram to sleep and performed his side of the deal in the form of smoke.

The covenant was "cut," as it was called, and every generation to follow was bound to experience the promises of it.

Throughout the rest of the Old Testament, we see the same covenant being repeated with the subsequent generations of Isaac and Jacob. All three were promised the blessing.

And we see the covenant come into full fruition through the life of Jesus. He was the one walking through the animal sides, he was the one cutting the covenant with Abram, and he was the one promising the blessing upon his genealogy.

Since you and I have been grafted into the seed of Abraham,[3] this covenant is still in play. We have been blessed to be a blessing to others. We are the ones standing on the side of the animals, acknowledging the covenant, agreeing with the terms and promises, and accepting all that God has to offer us.

You and I have been blessed.

And all the families of the earth are meant to be blessed through us.

Our commission is to spread the gospel message and make disciples of all the nations. Jesus says in John 13:35 (NLT), "Your love for one another will prove to the world that you are my disciples."

Is that true of the lives we are living?

Can people look at our actions and see that we are Jesus' disciples?

We must believe that our role is to be a blessing to all the families of the earth. It's our role to be a light and to be love to everyone. This is a major deal.

When I moved from Minneapolis to Charleston, I did the drive in one straight shot, twenty-four hours behind the wheel. I wouldn't recommend that for anybody.

I pulled into the stretch of townhouses just after sunrise. There were two people sitting on the patio above mine, but I couldn't see their faces.

At this point I was exhausted from driving through the night by myself. Since I only had one car's worth of stuff, unpacking was going to be easy. I didn't even have a bed, so I blew up an air mattress and put sheets on it.

As I was bringing in box after box and in a full-on sweat at this point, I overheard a deep voice from the patio above say, "Minnesota?! You're a long way from home, boy," and the person next to them started laughing.

I wasn't laughing. I was frustrated, exhausted, and a little overwhelmed because I had no idea what I had just gotten myself into.

Now, when I had called the police to ask about the neighborhood's safety before moving there, I'm not sure if the officer misunderstood me or what, but hearing gunshots that first night, I knew I was in for an adventure.

The next morning, I introduced myself to my neighbors on the way out the door. The deep voice from the day before was CeCe, and she was sitting with her adult daughter.

She had to have been 6 feet tall and 300 pounds, and she was a former truck driver from a small town in Georgia.

I was definitely a fish out of water down here.

The more I got to know CeCe, the more stories she shared about life on the road and life back at home. She told me about strangers visiting her hometown bars and causing trouble—so much so that one time it turned into a brawl and people started shooting each other.

I'm not sure if she was trying to impress me or if she was telling the truth. But I always sat there in agreement, pretending that I understood where she was coming from.

My neighbor in the townhouse to my left was a man named Patrick who had just gotten divorced and was trying to get back on his feet. Patrick owned a construction business that employed ex-cons and individuals who needed a little boost in life.

He also grew marijuana in his living room closet.

One of Patrick's best friends and employees was named Clyde. Clyde was one of those guys who looked much younger than he actually was, like I think he was in his fifties but he looked fifteen. And Clyde was tough. He was always bragging about how his police rap sheet, which outlined his arrests and convictions, was as long as he was tall, making it maybe 4 foot 11.

In their free time, Patrick and Clyde loved to go shrimping.

They told me about how they would catch a hundred pounds of shrimp in a night's work, and they gave me individually bagged portions that I'd toss in my freezer and eat every night after work.

But hearing the shrimping stories wasn't enough. I wanted to experience it for myself.

So one weekend, Patrick had me meet him at the grocery store before setting sail in order to pick up the supplies: rotisserie chicken, fish food, wet cat food, and menthol cigarettes.

At this point in my Charleston adventure, I had learned not to ask questions and just join in for the ride.

After the grocery store, we met at the marina to load up the boat. I was under the impression that Patrick, Clyde, and myself would be in a fishing boat of some sort, but Patrick pulled in with a little metal dingy that could barely hold the three of us, let alone a hundred pounds of shrimp. There was no room for extra movements, and thinking about the waves made me extra nauseous.

We loaded up the boat with our supplies and a handful of poles that had to have been ten feet long, and we took off to their secret shrimping spot.

Little did I know that shrimping is based on the tide, so as we waited for the tide to drop, we made "fish cakes," which consisted of fish food and wet cat food. The smell was horrendous. But this was their secret recipe, or so I was told.

When the tide dropped to its lowest, we drove in a line, tossing in a fish cake followed by one of those long poles to know where to go. We did this in a handful of places and then had to wait again for the tide to begin rising before we started the shrimping process.

Clyde ripped off a piece of rotisserie chicken with one hand as he held a cigarette in the other. He looked at me with his crooked smile and said, "Time to eat," passing me the chicken.

No plates. No silverware. Just three guys passing around a rotisserie chicken and pulling off pieces with our fish-food-caked fingers.

Supposedly shrimp also like to nibble on chicken bones, so we threw the leftovers on top of our marked territory.

As the sun began to set and the tide began to rise, it was our time to shine.

We pulled up to the first pole and tossed a shrimp net overboard. Pulling it back in, there was nothing there.

Second pole, same thing.

The third pole was a whole different story. Clyde tossed it overboard, and this time there were so many shrimp in his net that Patrick needed help to get it in the boat. We hit the mother lode. There had to have been five hundred shrimp in this one toss.

Over the next hour, it was jackpot after jackpot. We ended up hitting the legal limit of one hundred pounds of shrimp in a few hours of work. I was impressed and shocked at the same time.

After Jesus resurrected, he was standing on the shore of the Sea of Tiberias, looking at his disciples as they tossed net after net on one side of the boat without catching anything.

He called out to the disciples, "Throw your net on the other side of the boat!"

And even though they had been fishing all night without any luck, they proceeded to toss the net anyway.

This time was different.

Their net was so full of fish that it began ripping on the sides.[4] They had never seen such a load, and it all resulted from trying something different and seeing life through the eyes of another. Jesus knew a miracle was on the other side of the boat if they would just toss the net one last time in faith.

My time in Charleston lasted only six months before I decided to move back to Minneapolis and finish up my college degree. But my memories of CeCe and Patrick and Clyde will last with me for the rest of my life.

One of the best things we can do is learn to see life through the eyes of another person. As different as the four of us may have been from each other, we are all human beings, loved by God and created in his image.

So often we can look at people who are different from us and judge them for their lifestyle or the decisions they made. But maybe I would have made the same decisions if I had been in a similar circumstance.

The more I travel, the more I realize how unnecessary so many of our theological and social debates are. Every person is unique, so why do we think things can be black and white?

Professor J. Richard Middleton said it best: "Salvation does not erase cultural differences."[5]

We all see the world differently.

We all have different experiences.

I want to be open to others and surpass my comfort zone to dig into my curiosity, instead of judging and always thinking I'm right. Many things in life aren't black and white. There are a whole lot of gray areas. Our division is unnecessary and stifles our growth. Unity is the most important thing.

So let's love the entire human race. Instead of telling people why they're wrong, let's tell them who they are. Let's stand out and experience a new way of living.

There is a small lake close to my house that people love walking their dogs around. It's great exercise because from start to finish, you'll clock in about three miles in total.

On the south side of the lake is an ordinary tree with an extraordinary story. It's easy to miss if you are running by, but on the bottom of the tree is a small door with a gold door knocker and what looks like a mini garden surrounding the entrance.

It is the home of Mr. Little Guy, the elf.

Twenty-five years ago, a gentleman put a door on the tree because it looked cute. But then kids and adults alike began leaving gifts and letters for whoever "lived" there. So what else would the owner do than to write miniature letters back to them and sign the bottom with "MLG," for Mr. Little Guy.

He got all sorts of letters.

People sharing wishes and dreams.

Kids sharing Christmas lists.

A cancer diagnosis.

A close friend dying.

An engagement.

Lollipops.

Flowers.

There was no rhyme or reason behind the leaving of notes and gifts, but it helped countless lives.

For years I would write letters to Mr. Little Guy and leave him different gifts.

One year I left a beach ball, and MLG wrote back and told me how his daughter used the ball as a hot-air balloon to get across the lake. I would lie in bed at night dreaming about how cool it would be to be an elf and go on adventures that no other kids could imagine.

The kindness of one man in taking time to respond to people impacted countless lives.

People often describe loving others from the overflow of their cup, but I see it as a cup that's open on top and bottom.

We have blessings constantly being poured into our lives; instead of holding on to them, we can let them flow right through—in one side and out the other.

Jimmy Darts told me, "Whatever you have been allocated, you're responsible to redistribute to the people in your sphere, the people who you interact with each and every day. When God gives you something, it's meant to be enjoyed and shared in community, blessing other people from your blessing. The cool thing about it is that the more you realize this concept, the more you'll be given and the more often you can be generous. Doing that with the right heart can change the world."[6]

As we begin to realize that our whole life is a gift, the passing on of the blessings becomes our natural tendency. What goes in, goes out to help those around us.

If we focus on the Giver, we will give more.

We will never be a blessing if we're fixated on taking.

Always appreciate what you have been given. Benedictine monk David Steindl-Rast once said, "We tend to think that the happy people are grateful because they got what they like. In reality the grateful people are happy because they like what they got."[7]

Like what you got. This is all a gift. This is all for you to enjoy the master's happiness.

What are some other ways we can be a blessing to those around us?

Start with something simple, like buying a stranger's meal or coffee once a week.

Give something away.

Smile at others.

Be generous with your time.

IS THE WORLD A
BETTER PLACE TODAY
BECAUSE I'M IN IT?

IF NOT, GO OUT
THERE AND MAKE
IT HAPPEN!

Listen.

Ask yourself, is the world a better place today because I'm in it?

If not, go out there and make it happen!

You get to decide the story you tell. Let's make it an adventurous one.

CHAPTER 10

Speaking Life

IN 2014, I was diagnosed with anxiety.

Falsely.

The first time "it" happened, I was at work, waiting tables. I had just walked out of the kitchen with a tray full of food, heading toward Table 24, when all of a sudden I couldn't breathe.

My eyes widened. I cleared my throat. I did anything I could think of in the moment of panic to pull myself together, but nothing was working.

I whipped around and handed my tray to a co-worker. Without a word, I dipped out the back door for some fresh air in our alleyway.

That was weird, I thought, my hands still shaking from a nervous system on high alert.

After my shift, I went home confused about what had happened earlier, but I wrote it off as a one-time event.

Until it happened the next day. And the next.

All of a sudden, out of nowhere, my heart would start racing, my breathing would be shallow, my hands would start shaking, and I would freak out.

The third time it happened I went straight to the emergency room. The doctor ordered an EKG, but the results came back normal.

He said that I was having an anxiety attack and I needed to slow down.

"But I'm not an anxious person at all, it doesn't make sense. I was when I was a kid, but not any longer," I said.

He didn't want to hear it and was firm on his diagnosis. I wasn't anxious, though. There had to be something wrong with me that needed immediate attention. So after having another instance the following week, I booked an appointment with my primary doctor.

Blood test after blood test.

X-ray.

Hearing me out some more.

CAT scan.

At first he said I was prediabetic. Then he said I had mono. Then he realized he was wrong and there was nothing of immediate concern. I was simply having anxiety attacks.

I kept working at my job. Anxiety attacks.

I moved to Australia for a while. Anxiety attacks.

I moved to Miami. Anxiety attacks.

I finally accepted the fact that I was dealing with anxiety and began speaking it over my life: "I am an anxious person." But deep down I knew that wasn't true, because I was typically full of peace. And these "attacks" didn't happen all the time, only during certain times of the year. Yes, I had dealt with anxiety in social settings as a kid, but never like this. Something was off.

My mom also didn't agree with the doctors. She told me to pray about it, asking God to show me what was wrong. It had worked for her. The doctors couldn't figure out what was wrong with her once, so she prayed about it and woke up in the middle of the night with a strange word in her mind. She wrote it down and, the next day when she was in for testing, that exact word was the solution to her problem. It was a miracle. So she believed God would show me what was wrong. And I did too.

When I was living in Miami, the attacks heightened. I would be sitting by the pool when all of a sudden, *BAM!* I couldn't breathe. Or I would be in the gym and the same thing would happen.

As Gisela and I had been praying about the cause, she randomly suggested I visit an allergist.

"Maybe you're allergic to humidity," she said.

I responded with, "Huh? Is that a real thing?"

And then I began to think about it. Every single time I dealt with the attacks, it was in extremely humid conditions: Minneapolis summers, Australia, in the shower, Miami. She might be on to something here.

I booked an appointment for later in the week. We did test after test. They even did the one where you have like forty needle scratches in your arm and they put a bunch of oils on each scratch, looking for allergic reactions.

The results: Nothing.

Next up was the breathing test.

The results: Something.

I was allergic to humidity.

Well, not just humidity, but environmental changes in gen-eral, one of those being humidity.
How weird is that? But praise God, because now we had an answer! As you might know, there aren't many things worse than not knowing something and having speculation take charge of your life.

The doctor prescribed two nose sprays to take every morning, and they cleared me up completely. I haven't had a problem since. And it had nothing to do with anxiety.

Side note: When Gisela and I lived with my in-laws for a season, I would be so self-conscious taking my nose sprays after getting out of the shower every morning, because it sounded like I was snorting cocaine for break-fast. With my father-in-law in the next room, where he could hear everything, I would constantly remind him that I was taking my medication so he didn't get suspicious!

Humidity was the problem, and a simple medication was the solution. But when the doctor claimed I was anxious, I started thinking maybe I was, and began writing off situations as anxiety attacks, and questioning everything.

What has been spoken over you that is false?

Or what have you spoken over yourself?

The more you give attention to those things, the more they will stick around and try to convince you of their truth, when in reality they're a distraction.

Maybe it's that you are fearful.

Maybe it's that you are prideful.

Maybe it's that you aren't good enough.

Ask God what lie you are believing and confront it—whatever it is—because God didn't put that in you.

When you switch up your language and views of yourself, it changes everything. God says you are loved and talented and chosen. He created you to be special. You are one of one. There is nobody like you.

GOD SAYS YOU ARE
LOVED + TALENTED +
CHOSEN. HE CREATED
YOU TO BE SPECIAL.
YOU ARE ONE OF ONE.

When we begin to complain about who we are, we are essentially criticizing our Creator.

And that's a much bigger problem.

Life and Death

Nearly everything in life is influenced by words.

The greatest accomplishments in the world and the greatest evils. All of them begin, are developed, and are transformed through the words of various individuals.

I say the wrong words all the time.

I'll be eating at a restaurant by myself, and when the server asks if I need anything, I'll say, "No, we're fine, thank you," as I'm sitting there alone. Who am I with? My imaginary friend?

It was the worst when I was the one working in restaurants. I got so comfortable saying certain words that sometimes they would just slip out. Like one time when I was serving a woman and accidentally called her sir. How do you recover from that?

Bilingual people are fascinating to me—I only know one language, and I can barely handle that!

In Genesis, we see how God spoke things into existence, and later how his covenants impacted the world as we know it today.[1]

God's promises and Jesus' commissions influence our views of the future and what we do in the present, missionally.

The words we speak have massive implications for how we conduct our lives. Ultimately, we are responsible for our ability to perceive reality, and we, fundamentally, are the ones who determine it.

Our actions are one thing, but our words have the power to build or destroy. What we speak over someone's life can have a lasting impact.

The tongue is powerful.

In the wisdom literature from the book of Proverbs, King Solomon says, "The tongue has the power of life and death, and those who love it will eat its fruit."[2]

We have the ability to choose between good and evil with every word. For some of us, that's a difficult thing; for others, it's much easier. The Bible warns us to be cautious of every word that is freely spoken. And it says the reward will be high for those who use their words for good, love, justice, peace, and wisdom.

We have a choice every single day.

Deuteronomy 30:19 (NLT) says, "Today I have given you the choice between life and death, between blessings and curses. Now I call on heaven and earth to witness the choice you make. Oh, that you would choose life, so that you and your descendants might live!" We always have a choice. Life or death. Not that we would choose to die, but each one of our choices matters, bringing either life or death to the world around us, not just to us individually.

From how we love our neighbor to what we consume.

From how we respond under pressure to what we do with our money.

Every choice matters.

Every word we speak matters.

Everything brings either life or death.

In ancient literature, your name declared your purpose in life. God asks Adam to name the animals in the book of Genesis.[3]

There's a large, round, brown, hairy thing in front of him, and Adam says, "Bear."

Next up is a short thing with a circular shell, and he says, "Turtle."

He continues on with "woodpecker" and "sloth" and "rabbit."

Each name meant what they would become. Look up what your name means. Is it an accurate description of who you are?

In Exodus, we learn of an unnamed Hebrew baby who is sent down the Nile River in hopes of saving his life. The baby was found by an Egyptian princess who named him Moses.[4]

This is huge because in ancient Egypt, the name Mose or Mese translates to "of God," and was commonly paired with a specific deity. You would have Rameses or Thutmose, meaning "of Ra" or "of Thoth," respectively.

To have a generic Mose without a specific sponsoring deity is a complete political statement. Moses doesn't represent a specific deity, but at that portion of the narrative, he represents *the* God, who we later learn is named YHWH.

Renaming was a common practice in ancient literature. If your character is renamed, then your character has been charged with a new purpose. In this case, the Egyptian princess is providing a new identity for this forgotten Hebrew baby. And this name, Moses, transforms his very life; it adds complexity to his character.

Renaming includes the process of reimagining or calling upon a different narrative to help shift our perspective.

The story goes that when my family arrived in America from Sweden, their last name was Bengtson. But there were a whole lot of Bengtsons running around Superior, Wisconsin, and they wanted to stand out from the pack.

So the legend goes that my relatives went to a graveyard to find a new name, a new identity they could grow into while starting over in a new country.

And they chose the name Windahl.

In Scripture, we also see this with Simon, whose name meant "reed," being renamed Peter, meaning "rock."[5]

Or this strange story in Genesis 32, in which Jacob is wrestling with a man—some say it was an angel, some say it was Jesus. Either way, they were struggling with each other all night long.

The man says, "Let me go, for the day has broken."

Jacob responds with, "I will not let you go unless you bless me."

So the man said, "What is your name?"

Now, this is an important moment because previously Jacob had tricked his father into believing that he was his brother, Esau, in order to receive the blessing of the firstborn.

Jacob had lied about his identity for personal gain. And it bit him back. He ended up having to run away to begin a new life somewhere else.

So in this moment, when the man asked him his name, he is asking about Jacob's identity, who he really was inside. And after being worn out from wrestling all night, Jacob, known as a deceiver, responds honestly with, "I am Jacob."

He was now comfortable in his own identity.

The man responded with, "Your name shall no longer be called Jacob, but Israel."[6]

You see, Jacob in Hebrew means *supplanter*, "One who wrongfully or illegally seizes and holds the place of another."[7] Just as he did to Esau.

But his new name, Israel, means "wrestles with God," and it was at this moment that the nation of Israel was born. He was now walking in his true identity.

What has kept you from walking in your true identity?

Is it something that happened in your past?

Did someone wrong you, and you've been living with the consequences ever since?

Just as Abraham, Peter, Jacob, and others were renamed in the Scriptures, maybe you and I need to go through a renaming process as well, rewriting what has been spoken over our lives in order to walk in the true identity of who God says we are.

This doesn't mean you have to change your name; just start by saying, "I'm actually courageous and kind and patient."

At the moment when we do, we will be able to love others to the best of our ability.

Loving God and Loving Others

Toward the end of Jesus' life, he was asked, "Which commandment is the most important of all?"[8]

The timing of this question is important because he knew what was ahead. He knew death was right around the corner. When you're in that state, the details are no longer important.

Have you seen those pictures of old people holding signs on Instagram? They give their name, age, and one piece of life advice.

The advice is never about spending more time at work or focusing on dumb stuff; it's always about enjoying the moments you have with loved ones and being kind to others. Death is in the near future for them, and they're suggesting we focus on moments that bring us life.

When Jesus is asked this question shortly before his crucifixion, he stays in a similar lane. He says, "The most important is, 'Hear, O Israel: The Lord our God, the Lord is one. And you shall love the Lord your God with all your heart and with all your soul and with all your mind and with all your strength.' The second is this: 'You shall love your neighbor as yourself. There is no other commandment greater than these."[9]

Love God with all of you.

Love your neighbor as yourself.

That's it.

The entire Bible can be summed up in those two commands. Everything else is an explanation of that.

As new and revolutionary as these may be for some of us today, they were ingrained in the ancient Israelite tradition.

In the book of Deuteronomy, Moses is giving the younger Israelite people the Law before entering the Promised Land. The Law functioned as a handbook for how to live a holy life. In chapter 6, the author outlines the "greatest commandment" to the Israelite people, saying, "Hear, O Israel: The LORD our God, the LORD is one. Love the LORD your God with all your heart and with all your soul and with all your strength."[10]

Sound familiar?

This ancient community would pray this prayer every morning when they woke up and every evening when they went to bed. It's known as the *shema*, which is Hebrew for *hear* or *listen*, the first word of the prayer.

Hearing often indicated taking action in ancient texts, not just receiving a word that goes in one ear and out the other. The message is meant to be lived. How are you supposed to respond to the Lord being one? You should love him with all your heart and with all your soul and with all your strength.

Jesus would have prayed the shema twice every day. When you acknowledge your love for God twice a day, it shifts your perspective and keeps you focused on what is important in life.

As we grow in our love for Jesus, we become more loving to those around us through the Holy Spirit. It's a simple chain reaction. The more love we have, the more love we can give.

And God loves you so much, he's obsessed with you, which makes it so much easier to love him back. I mean, that's why we are Christians: "For God so loved the world that he gave his one and only Son, that whoever believes in him shall not perish but have eternal life."[11]

I'm loved by God.

You are loved by God.

Your Buddhist neighbor is loved by God.

Your Muslim neighbor is loved by God.

Your strange co-worker is loved by God.

Every single person from every nation and every language is wildly important in the eyes of God. Those people are our neighbor. It's our role to spread that love and let people know how to live life to the fullest, through a relationship with Jesus Christ.

I'm obsessed with movies about buried treasure.

There's just something about finding gold in an unexpected place that excites me.

My dad is the same way. But for him it has been a lifelong journey, beginning when he was a kid, climbing through my great-grandma's attic and flipping open dust-covered boxes to see what was inside.

A bandana here.

An old watch there.

Whatever he could find felt like it was more than enough.

His curiosity carried on through college, where he minored in archaeology and spent his extra time thumbing through old *Biblical Archaeology Review* magazines, becoming fascinated with the fact that the stories from the Bible were actually true, and you could see the findings in person.

Later in life he ended up producing a documentary film about the path of the exodus. This sparked an even greater passion for historical biblical evidence.

And his passion rubbed off on me.

The area I grew up in has a deep history to it, so one day my dad and I decided to rent a metal detector and see what we could find.

We loaded up the car with all of the supplies necessary for digging up our buried treasure: metal detector, a shovel, gloves, and an empty box.

And a whole lot of faith.

I suggested we go to the tallest hill we could find in the area, which happened to be in the middle of the woods. So we grabbed our gear and began hiking.

Once we reached our peak, I couldn't wait to start metal detecting, so I threw everything on the ground, turned on the metal detector, and started combing the area.

Literally, after one step it started going off.

Ping. Ping. Ping.

So we dug.

And about a foot down we found an old fork.

Then we found a rusty ax-head. And a knife. And more silverware.

After an hour of rummaging through the woods, we ended up with an entire trunk full of buried treasure. The bug inside of me was sparked. I loved exploring and coming across things you would never imagine finding, yet they were right below the surface.

How often do we fail to see the gifts that God has placed in us, just below the surface, yet other people see them so clearly? If you're like me, I can easily see how talented or smart or beautiful other people are, but sometimes it's hard for me to see those things about myself.

What would happen if we began to dig up the buried treasure hiding inside of everyone we come in contact with?

I want to show others God's love through encouragement and speaking life into their situation. Calling out who God made them to be.

It can be as simple as saying, "I love how you always see the good in every situation; it inspires me to do the same." We are called to build up others with our words instead of breaking them down. We have the choice to speak life or death with every word.

To bless someone means "to ask God to look favorably upon them."[12] If I believe God's way to be the best way, the most loving thing I can do is ask God to look favorably upon them.

And you know how good it feels when someone gives you encouragement? Especially when it's unexpected? Sometimes I struggle with accepting nice words, but I know that with every one of them, God is giving me a wink, saying, "That's how I feel about you too."

So tell somebody one encouraging thing this week. Start small. That one small comment could change their entire day, or life. If it's difficult to think of somebody, think of the person who encourages you most. Some people encourage all day long, but they're the ones who are often given the least encouragement. Go make their day.

The closer you get to God and the better you understand the Word, the easier it will be to see life from his perspective. We know he is good and just and loving and full of peace, so that's what we need to call out in people.

Bob Goff writes, "Instead of telling people what they want, we need to tell them who they are. This works every time. We'll become in our lives whoever the people we love the most say we are. God did this constantly in the Bible. He told Moses he was a leader and Moses became one. He told Noah he was a sailor and he became one. He told Sarah she was a mother and she became one. If we want to love people the way God loved people, let God's Spirit do the talking when it comes to telling people what they want."[13]

All of us who identify with and are followers of Jesus have been filled with the Holy Spirit, so co-creating alongside him should be our normal way of living. It's like every single day is a treasure hunt. We look for what God sees in someone and we pull it to the surface, whether they saw it inside of themselves or not.

I promise that you can find something nice to say about every person alive, so tell them. Let's leave every conversation better than it started. Let's speak life to ourselves and to those around us.

My senior year of high school I decided I was going to attend prom, even though I skipped the event the three years prior. I didn't have a girlfriend at the time, so I was really winging it when I chose to ask Grace because we had only talked once or twice.

Grace was on the basketball team, and that year our school was going to be in the state championship game. So that day at school, my friends and I were all dressed in fuzzy blue one-piece zip-up pajamas with blue face paint and bright yellow wigs.

Because what else would you wear during the state finals?

I had made a sign that morning that said, "Grace, Prom?" on it and stuffed the cardboard inside my outfit, anticipating the big reveal.

Little did I know that my friend Leah's mom had wrangled up the news media to come to the fan's section during halftime to get it all on camera.

Shortly before the second half of the game began, as the players were running back on the court, I lifted up my sign, and the people around me started chanting,

"Grace, prom."

Clap.

Clap.

Clap, clap, clap.

The chanting spread across the entire stadium, and all the news stations were dialed in on my face as I was standing with a dorky smile, contemplating all of my actions up until this point because I had no idea if she was even going to say yes.

But the support across the building was electric and gave me more courage than I knew what to do with.

I think every morning God is cheering us on like the stadium was cheering me. He believes in us and loves every moment that we spend living out our mission to love those around us.

He's chanting, "Goooo, Zach!"

Clap.

Clap.

Clap, clap, clap.

"Goooo, [your name here]!"

CHAPTER 11

Ripple

I GREW UP riding sideways.

Whether it was snowboarding, skateboarding, wakeboarding, or whatever, I was more comfortable running parallel than head-on.

My favorite sport was surfing. The only problem was that I lived in Minnesota. And I had never done it before. But I was obsessed with it. The culture, the freedom, the paradise, all of it.

I subscribed to *TransWorld Surf* magazine (before it went out of print, RIP). Even when I was riding any other type of board, I always pretended I was riding a surfboard. Any cement incline served as the perfect barrel wave.

When I moved to Australia at twenty-six, I was dead set on learning how to ride a wave, even if it was a tiny one.

I purchased a board my first day there. It was called the Vodka Cruiser, and it had an Asian-inspired sunset design. The funny thing about the name is that I'm actually allergic to alcohol. I know, humidity and alcohol. I guess God was protecting me from getting into trouble somewhere in the Caribbean.

My friends in Australia were real surfers. As much as you might pretend you're part of the culture, if you can't actually keep up, you're considered a poser. I was definitely a poser.

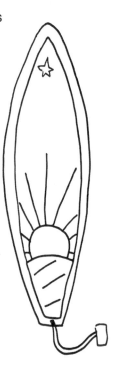

It was Christmas day, early morning.

A group of us met at our friend's house for breakfast. You know, eggs, peanut butter and white cheese, a little toast with Vegemite, typical Australian things. We were fueled up and ready to go.

The plan for the day was to hit Noosa, one of the most beautiful places in the world, just south of the Great Barrier Reef.

When we arrived, the beach was empty. A Christmas miracle.

Remember, I'm used to a whole lot of snow on Christmas day and playing hockey with my cousins all afternoon on the lake, not surfing in ninety-degree weather. But I was here for it.

Noosa had perfect waves.

Not a cloud in the sky.

The aqua glow bouncing off the rocks.

No seaweed washed up whatsoever.

There's no place like Noosa.

At this point in my surf career, I was three months in and yet to stand up. I loved it, though. Sitting on my board, rolling over the waves, timing them out in my mind. It was therapeutic.

Today was the day, though. I was going to ride a wave.

After failure after failure, my friend Kyle lent me his potato board.

It's a funny name for a board that's shaped like a potato and meant to be easier to ride.

And it did the trick.

I paddled out on Kyle's board. *This is it, I know it. Today is the day.* Once I got out far enough, I looked up at the sky. Clear blue with a generous portion of sunshine. I started kicking for dear life at the first wave that rolled in. . . .

And I caught it!

I stood up and rode all the way to shore. That moment was everything I could have ever imagined and more.

You know that feeling in your stomach when all is right with the world? Same thing here.

I continued to ride wave after wave for the rest of the day, a smile plastered to my face on each one. I was hooked.

The following week, the intensity of my schooling began to pick up, and I no longer had enough time to get out to the ocean, but my love for the sport never changed. And it wasn't just the surfing—it was everything having to do with the ocean and beach culture. I could sit and watch the waves come in for days and be happy as ever.

It's probably because that lifestyle often contradicts my life. It's hard for me to slow down. What's interesting is that the ocean is never still, so maybe I'm drawn to that aspect subconsciously.

There's an energy and a calmness clashing with every wave break.

Water by itself sits still. But energy moves through the water causing small ripples, which can eventually lead to gigantic waves.

The energy can come from a small gust of wind or something as major as an earthquake or volcano. Either way, a wave moves energy from one place to the next.

What began hundreds of miles away can transform into the perfect wave to surf.

Some people put up rocks or walls when they don't want the waves to pass through, but we don't want to be that guy. Let's create one ripple at a time that turns into inexpressible joy far, far away.

Making Waves

Everything in the universe is energy in motion, not just waves.

Our actions can cause ripple effects around our communities and can impact someone hundreds of miles away.

Think of it like this: Mandy has been struggling with her mental health for quite some time and is ready to give up. Life no longer seems to be worth living. One morning, as she's lost all hope, the person in front of her at the local coffee shop buys her coffee and says, "Have a great day!" with a smile. Nothing more, nothing less.

Mandy begins to question her thoughts and realizes there are some good people out there still.

With the feeling of generosity now inside Mandy, she decides to pay for lunch for the couple next to her, who seem to be having a fight. She even had her waitress slide them a note that said "Don't give up" on it. Little did she know that this couple was arguing over their potential divorce.

Mandy's one small act caused something to shift inside the couple and put a pause on the conversation. The next day was their thirtieth anniversary, and they were gifted a nice bottle of wine from the husband's best man, which caused them to reminisce about their wedding day.

Full of smiles, talking about the awkward moments and the sweet ones alike, the previous day's conversation on divorce was no longer in sight. They were present. And content. Maybe things would be tough again in the future, but for now, all was right.

The act of giving a cup of coffee rippled into saving a life, which rippled into further generosity that saved a marriage. You never know what one person is going through and how a simple act of kindness can completely transform a situation.

So often we focus on doing *big* things with our lives. What is one hug going to accomplish? Or one compliment? It might not do anything, but it might do a lot of things.

God is often found in the details, in the small things.

No matter how overwhelming the world may be or how many bad things are happening, one small act can start a ripple of change.

Jesus came to save the world by starting in a very small way. He started as a baby, was raised in the temple, worked hard at his job. There was nothing about him that screamed "Savior," according to his neighbors.

He was just a normal guy next door.

But as his purpose was revealed, he remained a servant, focusing on the small actions that create a major impact in the kingdom and in our lives. It was the small changes that started a ripple and eventually made waves throughout the world.

Jesus often used small, seemingly insignificant things to explain the kingdom of God.

> And he said, "With what can we compare the kingdom of God, or what parable shall we use for it? It is like a grain of mustard seed, which, when sown on the ground, is the smallest of all the seeds on earth, yet when it is sown it grows up and becomes larger than all the garden plants

and puts out large branches, so that the birds of the air can make nests in its shade."

With many such parables he spoke the word to them, as they were able to hear it. He did not speak to them without a parable, but privately to his own disciples he explained everything.

Mark 4:30–34

Jesus spoke about seeds.

And yeast.

Five loaves and two fish.

Flowers of the field.

Lost coins.

It was always the little things that mattered to Jesus.

We can get so caught up in being on the right side of theological debates that we miss out on the things that actually bring heaven to earth right here and right now.

We might not be able to solve world hunger alone, but we can buy a meal for a homeless person.

We might not be able to eradicate suicide, but we can check in on a friend.

We might not be able to lessen drug abuse, but we can take someone out to coffee.

Small acts matter a lot in the kingdom of God.

No, our salvation isn't based on works, but James writes that "faith apart from works is dead."[1] Doing nice things for your neighbor won't get you into heaven, but it will help them see Jesus within you. Paul writes in Ephesians 2:10, "For we are his workmanship, created in Christ Jesus for good works, which God prepared beforehand, that we should walk in them."

You and I were created for good works. Our actions matter. We never know what one small act could turn into.

I was on the practice green at a local golf course recently, which is where you go to practice chipping and putting. And I needed all the help I could get.

My friend James is an incredible golfer, and he was doing a few trick shots for fun. One of them is called the Tiger Woods shot, which became popular from a TV commercial a while back. You bounce the golf ball in the air a few times with your club then take a huge swing.

On this particular day, James had his club dialed in. Every shot was perfect. Until he did the Tiger Woods.

He was juggling the ball with the end of his club:

Bounce.

Bounce.

Bounce.

Then he wound up and hit the thing as hard as he could.

It was supposed to go down the fairway, but it went to the right instead. Our smiles froze in fear as we watched the ball fly across the street directly into the neighbor's bay window, completely shattering it from top to bottom.

Standing there with our eyes wide and jaws dropped to our ankles, the owner of the house came running outside yelling, "It's the #!@*&% from the golf course!" to his wife as he hopped in his car and came speeding into the parking lot.

Sometimes our intentions land where we want them to; sometimes they don't. What matters is that we keep on trying and do our best to not be the #!@*&% from the golf course.

The Torah contains 613 commandments, or *mitzvot*, to help the individual become closer to God. Most of these laws have been fulfilled through Jesus, so as Christians we are no longer held accountable for them, but there is still so much we can learn from them.

The word *mitzvah* (singular of *mitzvot*) often is related to an Aramaic word *tzavta*, which means "to attach or join."[2] In this sense, a mitzvah creates a bond between you and God, and the more you complete, the stronger your bond becomes.

The focus was on growing in your connection with God.

Over time, with the elimination of the sacrificial system, the Hebrew word *mitzvah* became synonymous with performing a good deed. So when you carry in your neighbor's groceries, you are performing a mitzvah, and in return living out a holy life.

Every one of our actions has a ripple effect and impacts the entire world, good or bad.

The earth crisis is a result of our actions, as are suicide rates, drug abuse, and war.

On the other hand, innovation is also a result of our actions. Same with women's rights, the civil rights movement, and electricity. All incredible things.

Our actions, big or small, play a major part in the future of society. One small thing can change everything for someone.

So start a ripple. Make a wave.

Here are some suggestions to get you started:

Buy a cup of coffee for the person behind you.
Pay for a couple's meal at a restaurant.
Give warm clothes and fresh socks to a homeless person.
Take a homeless person out to eat.
Serve at a homeless shelter.
Compliment a stranger.
Hand out flowers to people on the street.
Write a thank-you card.
Tell someone what they mean to you.
Plant a tree.
Pray for good things to happen to your family.
Buy someone's groceries.

Send a meal to a sick friend.

Donate to a crowdfunding page.

Leave your waiter a 100 percent tip.

Mentor a child.

Learn something new about a friend.

Eat locally grown foods.

Leave a positive review for a business online.

Save your extra change for a good cause.

Drink water, sleep eight hours, and work out.

Use reusable bags.

Write down five things you are grateful for.

Place encouraging post-it notes on your co-workers' desks.

Be kind to yourself.

CHAPTER 12

And Then You Breathe

I PROMISE I'm not narcissistic.

Sometimes I just do things because they make me laugh. And it's good to make yourself laugh. Let me explain.

I have a friend named Ethan who is one of the most creative and loving people I know. He's also a top-tier gift giver. For Christmas last year he sent me custom air fresheners with a picture of himself wearing an oversized fur coat on them. He's that type of gift giver.

And I laugh every time.

One day he forwarded me an ad on Instagram for a company that creates die-cut stickers with your face on them. Any sticker company could create face stickers, but this company knew how to market them. Ethan didn't even send me a message alongside the ad. He didn't need to; I was hooked.

So after living in Australia, I returned home to Minneapolis for a few years and ended up writing a book called *The Bible Study*. Most people are overwhelmed by the Bible, so I created a way to hold their hand as they read the entire thing. During the developmental stage of *The Bible Study*, I wanted our packaging to have unique features that made us stand out from other Bible study creators'. There aren't many independent ones, so my chances of standing out were pretty high.

Ethan had sent me the ad for the face sticker company the same week we were deciding what to do.

I immediately thought how funny it would be to put a sticker of my face, with a huge smile, on every box my company sent out the door of our warehouse. My lightbulb moment was to have the sticker be in the place of a return address label, the same place where you put the address in case the package doesn't make it back to its original destination.

Like, "This package needs to be returned, where do we send it?"

"Oh, we send it to this blond guy with the smile from ear to ear."

I printed a thousand of them.

The only reason was for my own enjoyment when thinking about the customer getting their order in the mail with a picture of me smiling on

the front of it. It wouldn't even have to be me, but it made sense because I wrote the book.

I still laugh thinking about it. Some people are weirded out or call me narcissistic, but it's still funny to me, and simple joys like that are worth the criticism.

When we first began shipping orders of *The Bible Study* with my face on it, a normal-sized mail truck would come to the warehouse every day and pick up a few copies to deliver to their destination. Our incredible warehouse team would send me a picture every single day of the orders going out in the mail truck.

Five sets a day.

Ten sets a day.

But then we started selling a lot of books.

Hundreds of sets a day.

Then thousands of sets a week.

The United States Postal Service went from sending a normal-sized mail truck to sending a van twice a day, to having to send a small semi-truck every afternoon to load up the pallets of orders.

And every single box had a sticker of my smiling face on it.

Our local post office, those poor people. Imagine making a daily pickup, touching hundreds of boxes with some guy's face on it. Our pickup person had no idea who I was because I lived in Miami at the time, and even if I visited the warehouse, our paths just never seemed to cross.

Her name is Cheryl.

One day it finally happened. At this point, Cheryl had probably moved tens of thousands of boxes with my face on them into her truck. Cheryl walked to the back of the warehouse, and we made eye contact. She knew who I was right away, so no introductions were necessary. I walked over to her, hugged her, took a deep breath, and just said, "Thank you."

Those deep-breath moments speak for themselves. Where all is at peace and the gratitude is overwhelming.

How do we get to a place like that with God?

Where we acknowledge how he's been working on things on our behalf for who knows how long,

and we take a deep breath,

and just say, "Thank you."

God in Every Breath

Our breath is about as basic as it gets.

When you are born, you begin to breathe.

When you die, you have taken your last breath.

Every single breath is a gift because it means you are alive. And it's a good thing to be alive.

We never own our breath. With each one, we are breathing in faith, hoping that oxygen will be there, but we don't own the oxygen. Breath itself is a gift that we are able to participate in because of God.

Take a breath yourself.

Breathe in.

Breathe out.

Each of those is something to be grateful for.

Earlier we talked about Moses at the burning bush in the book of Exodus. Think of how breathtaking that sight must have been for Moses—to see a bush that remained aflame, but also to be interacting with God for the first time. He had no idea who God actually was.

So after God explains to Moses all of the miraculous things he is going to do through him, Moses says,

> "If I come to the people of Israel and say to them, 'The God of your fathers has sent me to you,' and they ask me, 'What is his name?' what shall I say to them?" God said to Moses, "I AM WHO I AM." And he said, "Say this to the people of Israel: 'I AM has sent me to you.'" God also said to Moses, "Say this to the people of Israel: 'The LORD, the God of your fathers, the God of Abraham, the God of Isaac, and the God of Jacob, has sent me to you.' This is my name forever, and thus I am to be remembered throughout all generations."
>
> Exodus 3:13–15

In English we don't realize the significance of God's name, as it's often translated, "I AM WHO I AM." In Hebrew it's a different story. God has more than a thousand names throughout Scripture, but his one true name in Hebrew is "YHWH."

Jewish custom is to never say the name YHWH because of the holiness attached to it. Even though YHWH is in the Old Testament more than 6,800 times, they would skip over it and use replacement names instead.

Jewish culture revered God. And still does to this day.

Over time, the Christian tradition has added vowels to the name YHWH, pronouncing it "Yahweh," but at its simplest form with the individual letters Y H W H, it becomes a breath. We can't speak his name; we can only breathe it.

So whether you realize it or not, with every breath, you are speaking the name of God.

When you are sleeping, YHWH.

When you are eating, YHWH.

When you are depressed, YHWH.

His name is part of every moment, good or bad, he is always there.

No matter your age, race, gender, social class, city, state, country, whether you believe in God or not, he is there for you and available in every single breath.

In the beginning of the Bible, we are introduced to the Spirit of God, and he is hovering over the waters. If you remember, in chapter 3 of this book we talked about the

Babylonian creation story being about creation coming from within the chaos. But in Genesis 1, we see that the Spirit of God is hovering over the chaos and is at peace.

The Hebrew word for *spirit* is a complex word, *ruach*, also meaning wind and breath.[1]

God spoke, and new creation was formed.

He created land and said that it was good.

He created animals and said that they were good.

He created man and said that he was *very* good.

The same breath God used to speak is the same word for his Spirit. When God created Adam out of the dirt and breathed life into him, it was his ruach that was powering every breath, and it was his ruach that kept him alive.

God's Spirit is responsible for all creation.

In the ancient Hebrew tradition, their understanding was that God's ruach was the energy behind everything, moving all around us. Every gust of wind, every breath you take, every invisible action was powered by the overflow of God's ruach.

He is involved in all of it, and everything is controlled by Him.

His breath creates and his breath sustains.

It is all a gift.

And as big as he is, his desire is to be intimate with you. He chose you to be alive at such a time as this for a specific purpose. He loves you deeply and wants to be close through every breath.

Resurrection Life

Back in the time of Jesus, the temple was everything for the Jewish individual. It was a place where God's presence was believed to reside, and many religious acts were performed within the walls every day.

Prayer.

Sacrifices.

It was a place to show your dedication to God.

Shortly after Jesus' ministry began, during the time of Passover, Jesus went to Jerusalem to celebrate alongside the rest of the Jewish people.[2] But he became furious with what was happening within the temple, and he began flipping tables. These people were making sacrifices easy for the attendees instead of the process being real and from the heart. You could purchase a dove or a goat and not have to go through the process of raising it and thinking about the sacrifice throughout the year. It was a cheap fix to perform a religious duty instead of experiencing a heart transformation.

And God is always more concerned about our hearts.

So as Jesus is causing a ruckus, the leaders ask him why he thinks he has the authority to act this way. Jesus' response was, "Destroy this temple, and in three days I will raise it up."[3] The Jewish people laughed because it had taken forty-six years to create the temple, and they thought he was saying it would be built in three days. There was no way.

But Jesus wasn't talking about the temple; he was talking about his body. His death would not be the end—just the beginning.

Fast-forward to Jesus' execution and we see his statement came true: He rose from the dead three days later. Paul writes that it's the Holy Spirit who raised Jesus from the dead.[4]

It was God's ruach going back inside Jesus to create a new way of life. Things are no longer the way they were. Everything is different now. For them and for us.

Paul continues, "And if the Spirit of him who raised Jesus from the dead is living in you, he who raised Christ from the dead will also give life to your mortal bodies because of his Spirit who lives in you."[5]

As believers in Jesus Christ, we have been born again. God has breathed new life into us.

Do you really believe that the world is a terrible place and you can't wait to one day get out of here? Jesus' resurrection shows us that God hasn't given up on the world. He's redeeming everything back to the original plan. Resurrection is redemption available for all.

In John 20, Jesus is sitting in the Upper Room with his followers post-resurrection. The author says Jesus breathed on them and gave them the Holy Spirit.[6] I sure hope he had a first-century breath mint or something along those lines because there's nothing worse than when people breathe on me too close.

This moment is a tip of the hat to what we see in Genesis 2, when God breathed into Adam. This was another moment of new creation. Jesus was giving them life and life abundantly. He was sending them out into the world to spread the goodness of the kingdom in the same way he had just done for the previous three years. They were born again.

At Pentecost in the book of Acts we see the exact same thing. Jesus' followers are sitting around when all of a sudden a great wind, God's ruach, fills the room and deposits the Holy Spirit inside of them to begin spreading the good news of the kingdom of God.[7]

New creation was here through the resurrected body of Jesus and the born-again body we have been given. Yes, some things are awful in the world, but Jesus inaugurated the kingdom of God, and it's our role to help bring heaven into every moment. He promised to renew all things, not to blow it all up and transport us to another world.

In the future, God's plan will come to completion, but for now we have a job to do: to continue working his plan alongside him. We can taste it now.

Everything we do matters in the kingdom. Big or small. We are meant to bring hope and joy and peace and love and all sorts of goodness into every moment because we have the key to life. Your neighbors who don't know Jesus personally should have a great understanding of who he is based on the way you live your life.

The Holy Spirit's role is to transform you to be more like Jesus. The fruit you produce is supposed to look like his. Paul calls it the fruit of the spirit. It's God's ruach that is doing a new thing within you to create an even better thing all around you.

Our role is based around new creation, which begins with God's ruach and ends with God's ruach. His Spirit, his breath, his energy is powering all of life, and we have the opportunity to tap into it and help make our world a better place.

In his book *Surprised by Hope*, N. T. Wright writes,

> The point of the resurrection . . . is that the present bodily life is not valueless just because it will die. . . . What you do with your body in the present matters because God has a great future in store for it. What you do in the present—by painting, preaching, singing, sewing, praying, teaching, building hospitals, digging wells, campaigning for justice, writing poems, caring for the needy, loving your neighbor as yourself—will last into God's future.[8]

What we do now not only impacts the present, but also the future.

Jesus let us know that the kingdom of God is at hand; it's happening already. It will come fully into reality later, but we can tap into it now.

And we can tap into it by living more like Jesus every single day.

You Are Alive

For many people, life is something they're just trying to get through. It's tough. They need to work hard. Bad things often happen, and their only hope is that one day they will die and go to heaven.

For others, it's different. They understand how every breath is a gift from God, and he desires that we co-create the world alongside him. They have the ability to bring heaven into everything they do, and life is full of joy, even when their situation is hard.

Whichever basket you fall into, you have the choice of perceiving reality one way or the other. As it is said, you cannot control your circumstances, only your attitude. You can either give in and play the victim, or you can show others what my mom showed me. A resilient joyfulness at work within, a kingdom mentality that allows you not only to see the good all around you but to captivate others to want to see what you see.

Either way, you woke up today. That, in itself, is a miracle.

Take a moment right now to just breathe. Put both feet on the ground. And recognize each breath for what it is. A gift from God.

Breathe in.

Breathe out.

So often we tend to put wild expectations on our lives for no reason. We are stuck worrying about the future or thinking about the past. Anxiety overcomes us.

But Jesus is there for you in those moments too. In every breath you're speaking the name of God.

YHWH.

It can be so easy to just go about our days, but when we focus on being present, the cares of the world seem to diminish slightly.

There is a rose garden in Portland, Oregon, where various companies and wealthy people from all over the world grow personalized roses. Literally, one row is owned by a high-end fashion house, another is owned by a media mogul, while the rest are anywhere in between.

There are red roses and white roses and yellow roses and, really, whatever color rose you fancy.

The thing that makes the rose garden special is the soil. Botanists have found that this specific soil is the crème de la crème, the perfect pH level, calcium, and texture of dirt. To grow a rose there is better than anywhere else in the world.

And the garden sits right in the middle of the city—in the midst of the hustle and bustle, within arms' reach. Beauty surrounded by chaos.

At any moment people can stop and smell the roses, as cliché as the statement may be.

My friend Caleb wants to make his own type of rose one day, and I think that's the most beautiful thing. It would be the perfect reminder to stop all that we are doing, take a breath, and come back to reality.

You and I are here. Someone you love might not be. And one day, we too are going to die. But just as when my mom was near death and she was teaching me how life is a gift, I am inspired to live out that understanding one breath at a time. Because in reality, what a wondrous thing it is to be alive.

We are all part of something so much bigger than ourselves. Something we can't even begin to grasp. Something that could care less if someone cuts you off in traffic or you spill coffee on your shirt. So don't give those minor irritations a second of your attention—they're not worth it. Keep your eyes open to the beauty and wonder all around. And look up to God, and with a deep breath, just say, "Thank you."

That's where I'm at. That's what I've been feeling lately, whether it's right or wrong. At the end of the day, I want to be present and grateful and joyful and aware of God moving all around me. And I believe you play a big part in the world becoming more joyful as well.

I'm going to leave you with this quote from the late rabbi Abraham Joshua Heschel, who said, "Our goal should be to live life in radical amazement . . . get up in the morning and look at the world in a way that takes nothing for granted. Everything is phenomenal; everything is incredible; never treat life casually. To be spiritual is to be amazed."[9]

If we want true change, we must begin to see the good in every moment.

52 Gratitude Journal Prompts

1. List ten things you are grateful for.
2. What is one negative experience that turned into something good?
3. Name one person who has impacted your life without knowing it.
4. Who has impacted your life the most this year?
5. Name three people you are grateful for.
6. What is one accomplishment you are proud of?
7. How have you witnessed God move in your life recently?
8. What makes you feel at home?
9. What is one nice thing you have done for someone?
10. What is your favorite holiday?
11. What are you looking forward to?
12. What is the best part about the way you were raised?
13. Name your greatest life lesson.
14. If money were not an issue, what would you do with your time?

15. What is the nicest thing someone has done for you?

16. What is one thing you appreciate about yourself?

17. When have you felt the most courageous?

18. What item have you purchased that makes your life easier?

19. What was the best thing that happened this week?

20. How can you help others in your community?

21. What part of the day are you most grateful for?

22. Name one thing that made you laugh today.

23. Share your salvation story.

24. What is one talent you are most grateful for?

25. What is your favorite book or TV show? Why?

26. Name a teacher who has impacted your life.

27. What is one memory you will always cherish?

28. Name one thing that always makes you feel better.

29. List everything in your eyesight that you are grateful for.

30. What are you looking forward to most over the next ninety days?

31. What song has impacted your life most?

32. What is the best part about your job?

33. Who has made you smile the most this week?

34. What is the nicest thing someone has said to you?

35. What part of your body are you grateful for?

36. What are you struggling with right now? Can you find a silver lining?

37. What is the best news you have heard lately?

38. Name one person you can always count on.

39. Who inspires you to love others better?

40. Name one thing you are grateful for letting go of.

41. What makes you happy?
42. Describe your favorite place in the world.
43. What is your favorite meal?
44. How can you be more grateful?
45. What is the best gift you have ever received?
46. What basic necessity are you most grateful for?
47. Write about your most recent answered prayer.
48. What is one activity that brings you joy?
49. How can you be more generous (with time or money)?
50. What do people like about you?
51. When was the last time you felt at peace?
52. What do you love most about the season you are in?

A Special Thanks

Pete and T. Windahl for teaching me how to see the good, no matter the circumstance.

Caleb Brose, where to next?

Jeff Braun and Andy McGuire, let's go to Spoon again.

Sharon Hodge for making me sound way smarter than I am.

The entire Bethany House team for making us feel loved since day one.

Jesse Roberson, I owe you some wings.

Thomas de Armas-Wlodek for blowing my mind.

Bob for inspiring me to live a life of good stories.

Heather and the Choice PR girl gang, y'all rock.

Notes

Chapter 1: Shifting Our Perspective

1. Dylan Matthews, "23 Charts and Maps that Show the World Is Getting Much, Much Better," *Vox*, October 17, 2018, https://www.vox.com/2014/11/24/7272929/global-poverty-health-crime-literacy-good-news, and "Fact Question 9," *Gapminder*, http://gapminder.org.

See also Hans Rosling, et al., *Factfulness: Ten Reasons We're Wrong About the World—and Why Things Are Better Than You Think* (New York: Flatiron Books, 2018), 3–6; Johan Norberg, *Progress: Ten Reasons to Look Forward to the Future* (London: Oneworld Publications, 2016); and Steven Pinker, *Enlightenment Now: The Case for Reason, Science, Humanism, and Progress* (New York: Penguin Books, 2019).

2. Proverbs 11:14 NIV.

3. Proverbs 16:3 NLT.

Chapter 2: You Decide the Story

1. Kyle Bowe, "Your Odds of Being Alive," *Medium*, June 5, 2019, https://medium.com/afwp/your-odds-of-being-alive-af7826915073.

2. Robert Emmons, "Thanks! The Science of Gratitude," *The Table*, Biola University Center for Christian Thought, March 9, 2014, https://cct.biola.edu/thanks-science-gratitude/.

3. Sonja Lyubomirsky, "Pursuing Happiness: The Architecture of Sustainable Change," *Review of General Psychology* 9, no. 2 (2005): 111–113, http://sonjalyubomirsky.com/wp-content/themes/sonjalyubomirsky/papers/LSS2005.pdf. See also Caroline Leaf, *Switch On Your Brain* (Grand Rapids: Baker, 2015), and Mendel Kalmenson, *Positivity Bias* (New York: Ezra Press, 2019).

4. Dylan Matthews, "23 Charts and Maps that Show the World Is Getting Much, Much Better," *Vox*, October 17, 2018, https://www.vox.com/2014/11/24/7272929/global-poverty-health-crime-literacy-good-news. See

also Steven Dennings, "Why the World Is Getting Better and Why Hardly Anyone Knows It," *Forbes*, November 30, 2017, https://www.forbes .com/sites/stevedenning/2017/11/30/why-the-world-is-getting-better -why-hardly-anyone-knows-it/?sh=62e8fa757826; Julius Probst, "Seven Reasons Why the World Is Improving," BBC, January 10, 2019, https:// www.bbc.com/future/article/20190111-seven-reasons-why-the-world-is -improving.

5. Max Roser, "Most of Us Are Wrong About How the World Has Changed (Especially Those Who Are Pessimistic About the Future)," *Our World in Data*, July 27, 2018, https://ourworldindata.org/wrong-about -the-world.

6. Annie Kelly, "Gross National Happiness in Bhutan: The Big Idea from a Tiny State that Could Change the World," *The Guardian*, December 1, 2012, https://www.theguardian.com/world/2012/dec/01/bhutan-wealth -happiness-counts.

Chapter 3: New Creation

1. Joshua J. Mark, *Enuma Elish—The Babylonian Epic of Creation*, World History Encyclopedia, May 4, 2018, https://www.worldhistory.org/article /225/enuma-elish—-the-babylonian-epic-of-creation—-fu/. See also Tim Mackie and Jonathan Collins, Ancient Cosmology series, *BibleProject* podcast, May 2021, https://bibleproject.com/podcasts/the-bible-project -podcast/.

2. Walter Brueggemann, *Genesis: Interpretation: A Bible Commentary for Teaching and Preaching* (Louisville, KY: Westminster John Knox Press, 1986), 24.

3. Genesis 1:28 NIV.

4. Luke 1:41.

5. See Shoshanna Lockshin, "What Is a Mikveh?," My Jewish Learning, https://www.myjewishlearning.com/article/the-mikveh/.

6. See Luke 3:1–22.

7. Luke 3:16.

8. Matthew 3:16–17.

9. See also G. K. Beale and Mitchell Kim, *God Dwells Among Us: Expanding Eden to the Ends of the Earth* (Downers Grove, IL: InterVarsity Press, 2014).

10. N. T. Wright, *Simply Good News: Why the Gospel Is News and What Makes It Good* (New York: HarperCollins, 2015), 97.

11. See Philippians 3:20.

12. See Tzvi Freeman, "What is Tikkun Olam?" Chabad.org, https://www.chabad.org/library/article_cdo/aid/3700275/jewish/What-Is-Tikkun-Olam.htm.

Chapter 4: Shabbat

1. See Exodus 20:8–11.

2. See also Walter Brueggemann, *Sabbath as Resistance: Saying No to the Culture of Now* (Louisville, KY: Westminster John Knox Press, 2014).

3. Exodus 20:2.

4. See Karl Barth, *Church Dogmatics: The Doctrine of Creation*, Volume 3 (New York: Bloomsbury Publishing, 2004).

Chapter 5: It's a Celebration

1. Joseph Pieper, *In Tune with the World* (South Bend, IN: St. Augustine's Press, 1999), 62.

2. Deuteronomy 14:25–26.

3. See Matthew 11:19; Luke 7:34.

4. See also Tim Chester, *A Meal with Jesus: Discovering Grace, Community and Mission Around the Table* (Wheaton, IL: Crossway, 2011), and Norman Wirzba, *Food and Faith: A Theology of Eating* (United Kingdom: Cambridge Printing House, 2019).

5. C. T. McMahan, "Meals as Type-Scenes in the Gospel of Luke," PhD dissertation, Southern Baptist Theological Seminary, 1987, as quoted in Craig L. Blomberg, *Contagious Holiness: Jesus' Meals with Sinners*, ed. D. A. Carson, vol. 19, *New Studies in Biblical Theology* (Downers Grove, IL: InterVarsity Press, 2005), 163.

6. See John 2:1–12.

Chapter 6: He's Way Funnier in Real Life

1. See Isaiah 61:10; Matthew 25:21; Luke 10:21; John 15:11; 17:13; Hebrews 1:8–9; 12:2.

2. Jeremiah 1:5; Psalm 139:14; Matthew 6:8.

3. See Elton Trueblood, *The Humor of Christ: A Bold Challenge to the Traditional Stereotype of a Somber, Gloomy Christ* (New York: Harper-Collins, 1964). See also Henri Cormier, *The Humor of Jesus* (New York:

The Society of St Paul, 1977), and Earl F. Palmer, *The Humor of Jesus* (Vancouver: Regent College Publishing, 2001).

4. Luke 2:10.

5. Galatians 5:22–23.

6. John 15:11.

7. G. K. Chesterton, *Orthodoxy*, Centennial Edition (Nashville, TN: Sam Torode Book Arts, 2008), 158.

Chapter 7: Feel All the Feels

1. Matthew 28:17.

2. Matthew 28:20.

3. David G. Benner, *The Gift of Being Yourself: The Sacred Call to Self-Discovery* (Downers Grove, IL: InterVarsity Press, 2015), 41.

4. Timothy J. Keller, *Joy*, a sermon preached on April 8, 2010 from Romans 5:1–11 in *The Timothy Keller Sermon Archive* (New York: Redeemer Presbyterian Church, 2013).

5. Keller, *Joy*.

Chapter 8: See the Good

1. See James 1:17.

2. See Summer Allen, PhD, "The Science of Gratitude," Greater Good Science Center at UC Berkeley, May 2018, https://ggsc.berkeley.edu/images/uploads/GGSC-JTF_White_Paper-Gratitude-FINAL.pdf.

3. Allen, "The Science of Gratitude."

4. Luke 17:11–14.

5. Luke 17:14–16.

6. Luke 17:17–19.

7. See Exodus 3.

8. Rabbi Shelly Barnathan, "D'var Torah: Turning in Order to See," Philadelphia Jewish Exponent, January 7, 2021, https://www.jewishexponent.com/2021/01/07/turning-in-order-to-see/.

9. Alice Walker, *The Color Purple* (London: Penguin Books, 2019), 195.

10. Richard Foster, "The Art of Celebration," *Boundless*, November 23, 2006, https://www.boundless.org/faith/the-art-of-celebration/.

Chapter 9: How to Be a Blessing

1. See Romans 2:4.

2. Genesis 12:1–3.

3. See Romans 11:17.

4. See John 21:3–6.

5. J. Richard Middleton, *A New Heaven and a New Earth: Reclaiming Biblical Eschatology* (Grand Rapids, MI: Baker Academic), 174.

6. Personal interview with Jimmy Kellogg.

7. David Steindl-Rast as quoted by Esther de Waal, *Living with Contradiction: An Introduction to Benedictine Spirituality* (New York: Morehouse Publishing, 1997), 142.

Chapter 10: Speaking Life

1. See Genesis 1; 12:1–3.

2. Proverbs 18:21 NIV.

3. See Genesis 2:19–20.

4. See Exodus 2:1–10.

5. See John 1:42.

6. See Genesis 32:22–32.

7. "3290. Yaaqob," *Strong's Concordance*, Biblehub.com, https://biblehub.com/hebrew/3290.htm, and "supplanter," *The Free Dictionary*, https://www.thefreedictionary.com/supplanter.

8. Mark 12:28.

9. Mark 12:29-31.

10. Deuteronomy 6:4–5 NIV.

11. John 3:16 NIV.

12. "Bless," *Lexico*, https://www.lexico.com/en/definition/bless.

13. Bob Goff, *Everybody Always: Becoming Love in a World Full of Setbacks and Difficult People* (Nashville, TN: Nelson Books, 2018), 31.

Chapter 11: Ripple

1. James 2:26.

2. Tzvi Freeman, "What Is a Mitzvah?" Chabad.org, https://www.chabad.org/library/article_cdo/aid/1438516/jewish/Mitzvah.htm.

Chapter 12: And Then You Breathe

1. See also Tim Mackie and Jonathan Collins, Holy Spirit series, *BibleProject* podcast, March 2017. *BibleProject* podcast, May 2021, https://bibleproject.com/podcast/series/holy-spirit-series/.

2. See John 2:13–22.

3. John 2:19.

4. See Romans 8:11.

5. Romans 8:11 NIV.

6. See John 20:22.

7. See Acts 2:1–13.

8. N. T. Wright, *Surprised by Hope: Rethinking Heaven, the Resurrection, and the Mission of the Church* (New York: HarperOne, 2008), 193.

9. Abraham Joshua Heschel as quoted in Erica Brown, *Take Your Soul to Work: 365 Meditations on Every Day Leadership* (New York: Simon & Schuster, 2015), 5–6.

Author and entrepreneur **Zach Windahl** has helped thousands of people better understand the Bible and grow closer to God through his company, The Brand Sunday. He's the author of several books, including *The Bible Study*, *The Best Season Planner*, and *Launch with God*. Zach lives in Minneapolis, Minnesota, with his wife, Gisela, and their dog, Nyla.

More from
Zach Windahl

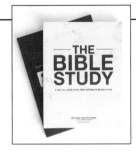

Reading the Bible can feel overwhelming. *The Bible Study* helps you journey through the Word while relating to and retaining the Scripture like never before! This impactful and approachable resource includes a motivating one-year study, daily and weekly guidance, and thought-provoking questions to strengthen your relationship with God.

The Bible Study

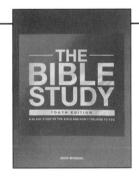

Written for middle-schoolers and high-schoolers, this 90-day study takes you through each book of the Bible with an easy-to-follow framework that helps you better understand the Bible and feel confident in your faith. Transform your life from the inside out while you discover new and exciting ways of connecting to the Word.

The Bible Study: Youth Edition